WILLIAM E. WARREN

THE SCREAMING SKULL
True Stories of the Unexplained

Illustrated by Neil Waldman

Prentice-Hall Books for Young Readers
A Division of Simon & Schuster, Inc., New York

Published by Prentice-Hall Books For Young Readers
A Division of Simon & Schuster, Inc.
Simon & Schuster Building
1230 Avenue of the Americas
New York, New York 10020
Prentice-Hall Books for Young Readers is a trademark
of Simon & Schuster, Inc.
Designed by Constance Ftera
Manufactured in the United States of America

10 9 8 7 6 5 4 3 2 1

Library of Congress Cataloging-in-Publication Data

Warren, William E., 1941-
    The screaming skull.

    Summary: Presents fourteen accounts of documented,
mysterious occurrences involving ghosts, poltergeists,
unexplained appearances and disappearances of people,
as well as unexplained mysteries such as the Shroud
of Turin.
    1. Curiosities and wonders—Juvenile literature
[1. Curiosities and wonders. 2. Occult sciences]
I. Waldman, Neil, ill. II. Title.
AG243.W375 1987   031'.02   87-6909

ISBN 0-13-796699-7

For Kitty Peterson,
who is six persons combined in one:
wife
mother
journalist
teacher
author
and most of all, a true friend

CONTENTS

THE SCREAMING SKULL

INTRODUCTION

IT HAS BEEN SAID THAT "TRUTH IS STRANGER THAN FICTION." INDEED, the real world around us is stranger than we can possibly imagine. But even as we struggle to understand our world, we find other worlds of mysterious, unexplainable events that lie just beyond our grasp.

We can put a man on the moon—but we cannot explain how or why a man named David Lang disappeared forever one sunny day while standing in full view of five people who knew and loved him.

We can split the atom and produce nuclear energy—but we cannot explain how a nuclear-type explosion occurred in Russia in 1908, thirty-seven years before nuclear power existed on earth.

We can accurately chart the land and the seas around us—but we cannot understand how, in 1513 A.D., a Turkish admiral was able to accurately chart unexplored lands and seas that no man, including himself, had ever seen.

Science tells us that all natural events have natural causes—and we agree. But what about unnatural events? Do they, too, have natural causes? If an event could not possibly occur, yet it occurs anyway and under impossible conditions, what then? Do we merely say that, because the event cannot be explained in natural terms, it did not happen?

Consider, for instance, the Maco Station Light. This eerie light has been seen regularly at night for more than a hundred years by countless thousands of witnesses, including scientists who have studied it and photographers who have taken pictures of it. Yet no one has ever been able to suggest any plausible explanation for the light's existence. Does this mean that the light does not exist, or that the thousands of witnesses have been wrong? It seems unlikely.

Or take the case of Barney and Betty Hill. What happened to this middle-aged couple on the night of September 19, 1961, simply could not have occurred—yet it did!

The fourteen accounts in this book are unusual, bizarre, and often unbelievable—but they are also true. They have been grouped into three sections: *true ghost stories, strange appearances and disappearances*, and *unexplained mysteries around us*.

The first section of the book, true ghost stories, is devoted to five brief excursions into the supernatural world of ghosts and spiritualism.

The second section contains five incredible-but-true stories of people who have appeared or disappeared in an eerie, baffling manner.

The third section investigates four of the most fascinating unexplained mysteries known to humanity.

All of the stories except one ("An Unfinished Ghost Story") are well known. Some are quite old; others are as recent as this morning's newspaper. But all of these events, although unexplained, are real. They actually happened to ordinary people on what started out as ordinary days.

So if you find yourself becoming confused as you read about the Shroud of Turin, the Nazca Lines, the lost colony of Roanoke, or the screaming skull of Anne Griffith, don't worry. You aren't alone. No one else knows exactly how or why these events occurred, either—but they did occur.

Even if we cannot understand or explain the mysterious forces that sometimes change normal, everyday events into supernatural occurrences, we can still enjoy reading about them.

We can wonder about them, and accept them simply as unexplained mysteries—because that is precisely what they are.

True Ghost Stories

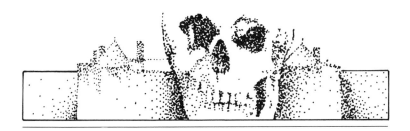

THE SCREAMING SKULL

OF ALL THE STATELY AND HISTORIC HOMES IN ENGLAND, NONE IS more lovely or mysterious than Burton Agnes Hall. Located in the East Riding section of Yorkshire, the ancient, three-story Elizabethan mansion has for many years been the home of the Boynton family.

Since the 1600s, the Hall has also been the home and final resting place of a human skull—a skull that has filled the night air with frightful screams and shrieking whenever it has been removed from the Hall.

The mansion known as Burton Agnes Hall was already centuries old when its owner, Sir Henry Griffith, died sometime during the last years of the reign of Queen Elizabeth I (1558–1603). Upon Sir Henry's death, ownership of the vast Burton Agnes estate passed to his three daughters, none of whom was married.

The sisters were proud of their family home. They had lived

in Burton Agnes Hall all their lives, and they loved it very much.

Now, with the great wealth they had inherited, the three women decided that the Hall should be rebuilt on a grander scale, with all of the latest features in architecture and furnishings. They would make Burton Agnes Hall the finest mansion in all of England. They hired the most famous architect in the world—an Englishman named Inigo Jones—to draw up plans for their desired changes. Then they commissioned one of the greatest painters in history, Peter Paul Rubens, to design and decorate the interior of the mansion. The cost of all the work was staggering, but for the sisters it was well worth the expense. They could easily afford to hire the best workmen and buy the finest materials in order to realize their dreams for Burton Agnes Hall.

Among the Griffith sisters, none was more deeply involved in the rebuilding project than Anne, the youngest of the three. From the beginning Anne worked day and night with boundless energy, planning the changes to be made, buying expensive decorations, furniture, paintings, and sculpture, and constantly searching for ways to make their home even more beautiful.

And when at long last the work was finished and the mansion was completely restored, none of the sisters was prouder of their new home than Anne. She loved to walk about the mansion, admiring its breathtaking treasures and matchless beauty. Her whole life was, in fact, one of loving devotion to Burton Agnes Hall. It was the house she was born in—and as we shall see, it also was the house she would die in.

Not long after the work was completed and the sisters moved in, Anne decided one afternoon to visit some neighbors who lived a short distance away. She informed her sisters of her plans, and told them that she would be back before dark. They warned her to be careful of tramps and robbers who were known to be in the area. Anne was not afraid: she often took long walks in the afternoon, and she had never been bothered by vagabonds or thieves. At her sisters' urging, however, she took along her pet dog to keep her company on the road.

She set out in high spirits along the road leading to Harpham. Her neighbors, the St. Quentin family, lived about a mile away.

Anne met no one until she came to an area known as St. John's Well. There she saw two men dressed in beggars' rags. They were lying on the grass by the roadside, apparently asleep. They awakened at the sound of Anne's dog barking at them, rose, and brushed themselves off. One of the men, who carried a walking stick in one hand, asked Anne to give him some money. She reached into her purse and drew out a few coins.

As Anne extended her hand toward the man, he spied an expensive ring on her finger. He demanded that she give him the ring as well.

Anne's eyes widened in horror.

"I cannot give you the ring," she protested. "It was my mother's ring; it has been in our family for many years. My mother wore it until shortly before she died, when she gave it to me. I have worn it ever since."

The other beggar stepped forward, eyeing the beautiful ring and grinning cruelly. "And you will die, too, milady, if you do not give it to us."

"Be quick about it," the first man said harshly, reaching for the ring, "lest we be forced to take it off your finger. We mean to have that ring for ourselves!"

"No, you cannot have it!" Anne cried. She began to scream, and her dog barked furiously as the men struggled with her for possession of the ring.

"No one can hear your screams, milady," grunted one of the beggars. But Anne continued to struggle and cry for help until finally the man gave her a vicious blow on the head with his walking stick. She slumped to the ground, unconscious. The thieves snatched her ring and ran away.

When Anne was found some time later, lying senseless where she had fallen, she was taken to the St. Quentin family's home, where she was cared for while her sisters were notified of her accident. The next day they took her home to Burton Agnes Hall.

At first her health seemed to improve slightly. She regained consciousness, but even with her sisters' constant care and attention she never recovered from the blow to her head. After five days, knowing that death was not far away, Anne called her sisters to her bedside.

"From birth have I loved this house," she told them, "and in death I would not gladly leave it. My fate and the fate of this house are bound together. Promise me that, when I am dead, I will not be wholly separated from this house that I love as much as life itself."

"What would you have us do, Anne?" one of her sisters whispered tearfully.

"I wish to have my body placed in the family vault in the churchyard," Anne replied calmly, as if she were discussing events of no more importance than the weather. "But I wish to have my head removed from my body and kept in this house forever. Never let it be taken away or buried apart from this house. This is my last wish, which I pray you to fulfill when I breathe no more."

Then, seeing the look of shock and horror on her sisters' faces, she added, "I ask you, my sisters, to honor my wishes, and to make my request known as well to future generations of owners of Burton Agnes Hall. If they forget or disobey this, my last wish, my spirit will return to disturb the house. I will make it uninhabitable for its owners."

Anne's sisters considered that her strange words were merely the result of her severe head injury. They had no intention of carrying out her bizarre request—but in order to comfort her in her last hours, they agreed to fulfill her wishes.

She died peacefully a short while later. Her body—including her head, which had not been severed and preserved as she had requested—was buried in the family vault.

In the weeks that followed Anne's funeral, strange things began happening inside Burton Agnes Hall. A loud crash was heard in an upstairs room, but servants who investigated the noise found nothing disturbed in the room.

One night everyone in the house was awakened by the sound of doors slamming shut. But as quickly as people reached one door that had closed with a crash, they heard other doors slamming shut in other parts of the house. They followed the sounds from place to place, finding doors closed and in some cases locked securely, until at last, after several hours of such activity, the disturbances ended. The searchers went back to bed, weary and frightened. No one slept in Burton Agnes Hall during the remainder of that long and frightening night.

The next week, the sisters and others in the house began hearing heavy, running footsteps in the empty hallways outside their rooms after they went to bed. And if that were not enough to terrify them out of their wits, they heard unearthly groans and blood-curdling screams echoing down the dark halls and lonely corridors, as though someone were suffering unbearable pain and agony.

By now the sisters recalled Anne's dying words: *If they forget or disobey this, my last wish, my spirit will return to disturb the house. I will make it uninhabitable for its owners.* They wasted no time in consulting the vicar, or minister, of Burton Agnes. They told him about the eerie sounds in the night, and confessed that they had not complied with their dying sister's wish to have her

head preserved within the Hall for all time. The vicar advised them to have Anne's coffin re-opened for examination.

When the coffin was dug up and the casket opened, Anne's body was just as it had been at her death—but her head was rotted away to a grinning skull. Worse, her skull had been severed from the rest of her body, although her head and body had been intact when she was buried.

No one could account for these extraordinary discoveries. The astonished vicar decided that supernatural forces were at work. He declared that Anne's soul would find no peace until her skull was returned to Burton Agnes Hall, and he suggested that the sisters act immediately to satisfy her last wishes. They quickly took his advice and brought Anne's skull back to the Hall. They set it in a place of honor on a table where it remained, prominently displayed for all to see, for a number of years. And as long as the skull lay undisturbed inside the house, no further night sounds or disturbances plagued Burton Agnes Hall.

The Return of the Screaming Skull · After the last of the Griffith sisters died and ownership of Burton Agnes Hall and its estates passed to the Boynton family in 1618, a maid at the mansion decided to get rid of the ghastly skull. When no one else was around, she sneaked into the room where the skull was displayed and tossed it out an open window. It landed in a passing horse-drawn wagon that was filled with straw.

When the skull landed in the wagon, the horses stopped suddenly. No amount of urging or whipping by their owner could move them: it was as if they were mired in deep mud and unable to move forward or backward to free themselves.

Eventually, the owner of the wagon discovered the skull lying in the straw. And when the affair finally was resolved and the skull was returned to its previous resting place in the Hall, the horses calmly went on their way without further ado.

By this time, everyone in the area knew of the curious stories surrounding "Awd (Old) Nance," as they referred to Anne. Still, not everyone (including some of the Boynton family) *believed* the stories.

Once, a member of the family had the skull taken outside and buried in the garden behind Burton Agnes Hall. After a sleepless night spent cowering beneath his bedcovers, listening to the agonized screams and anguished shrieks that filled the night air, the lord of the estate quickly had the skull returned to the Hall.

Yorkshire residents said that the restless ghost of Anne Griffith could be seen prowling the lonely halls and corridors of Burton Agnes Hall at night whenever the skull was moved from one room to another. But sometime around 1900, the owner of the Hall had the skull bricked up within a wall in the mansion in order to prevent its being removed. Since that time, nothing further has been heard from the screaming skull of Burton Agnes Hall.

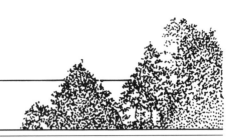

THE GHOST LIGHT
AT MACO STATION

In 1867, Joe Baldwin was a railroad conductor working for a company which later became the Atlantic Coast Line Railroad. Joe was a model employee: he was deeply loyal and devoted to the company, and also to the train he worked on. He loved his work so much that he didn't really mind the long hours he spent on the job.

The train Joe served on as conductor had an old wood-burning locomotive that was built long before the Civil War began. It made regular passenger runs between Wilmington, North Carolina, Florence, South Carolina, and Augusta, Georgia. Besides tending to the needs and comforts of his passengers, Joe Baldwin's job included keeping the coaches clean and free of the inky black soot that was produced by the engine and poured out by the smokestack. It was not an easy job, but Joe was a tireless worker.

One rainy spring night in 1867, the train was nearing the end of a return trip from Augusta to Wilmington. It had been a long trip, and a tiring one. Joe was happy, though: the train was right on schedule, and soon he would be home with his family again.

But Fate has a way of playing strange (and sometimes cruel) tricks on people. This time, as the train puffed and chugged its way eastward, homeward bound in the dark, rainy night, Joe Baldwin was about to become a victim of the cruelest fate of all.

Fourteen miles west of Wilmington, North Carolina, lies the tiny community of Maco. In 1867, though, there was only a small, unimportant railroad station house to mark the spot. Known as Maco Station, it was a single building in a small clearing that had been hacked out of the surrounding forest of scrub pines and underbrush along the railway line.

As the locomotive reached a point a few miles west of Maco Station, Joe checked his pocket watch. It was time to alert the passengers that soon their long trip would be over. They were less than twenty miles from Wilmington.

Suddenly, Joe sensed that the train was slowing down slightly. He wondered what was wrong. No such slowdown was scheduled for the Maco Station area. Hurrying to the leading passenger coach, he arrived in time to see the front section of the train moving away quickly into the night. Somehow, the passenger coaches had become uncoupled from the rest of the train!

Then, as the engine disappeared and its noise faded into the distance, another, terrifying sound arose from the opposite direction: the long, mournful whistle of another train coming up behind them from the west.

Joe Baldwin grabbed his lantern and raced through the passenger cars toward the rear of the train. As he went, he shouted for the passengers to leave the train immediately, although the cars were still moving at a fairly rapid rate of speed.

When Joe reached the end of the train, he burst through the door and onto the platform at the rear of the car. He could see clearly the bright, single headlight of the approaching train. It was no more than a few hundred yards away now, and growing ever larger as the train raced toward him.

He had to warn the engineer, he thought wildly. The man didn't know that the passenger cars had become uncoupled and were slowing down; unless someone did something, and right now, a terrible train wreck would occur!

With no thought for his own safety, Joe Baldwin began swinging his lantern frantically back and forth, trying to signal the engineer. But either the engineer didn't see Joe's lantern, or else it was too late for him to stop his train before it plunged into the drifting passenger cars. With a grinding crash, the oncoming locomotive plowed at full speed into the rear of the car Joe was signaling from.

The night suddenly erupted in a fury of metal screams and thunderous crashes. Train cars were bounced and tossed around the tracks like a child's toy train as the passengers scattered toward safety.

Joe Baldwin died instantly in the crash. His head was ripped away from the rest of his body. Witnesses at the scene later said that the conductor's last act before the train collided with the passenger cars was to toss away his lantern. It landed a short distance away in a marshy area beyond the rails. But it never went out. It continued to burn brightly, as if to remind the witnesses that some things never die.

Naturally, the train wreck at Maco Station attracted curious visitors to the scene of the accident. Soon, many of those visitors were reporting the appearance at night of a strange, ghostly light that was as mystifying as it was frightening. And as its fame spread along the eastern coast, the eerie light became known far and wide as the Maco Station Light.

Like North Carolina's other famous, unexplained light which shines over Brown Mountain, the Maco Station Light has been seen by many thousands of people over the years since it first appeared.

However, the Maco Station Light is far more regular in its appearances than western North Carolina's mystery light has been. Especially in the spring and summertime, and on cloudless, moonlit nights when the sounds of crickets chirring and bullfrogs croaking fills the air, it is not at all uncommon for the Maco Station Light to make as many as twenty-five to thirty appearances in a single evening at regular intervals.

Witnesses say that the appearances are always the same. Gathered along the tracks and looking west, observers see a small light flickering in the darkness. At this point, the light appears to be about a mile away, hovering a few feet above the left rail.

Then, without warning, the light grows larger and brighter, like a fiery white or yellow moon. It begins to glide silently and swiftly along the tracks toward Maco Station. As it rushes toward the shocked observers, it swings back and forth like the pendulum of an old grandfather clock. (Or, some people say, like the lantern waved by Joe Baldwin on that fateful night in 1867.)

The watchers, who often come in groups by the carload to view the eerie event, look on in stunned silence, or else they utter small gasps of surprise as the light looms larger and larger in front of them.

And then, just as suddenly as it began, the light comes to an abrupt halt a football field's length away from the nearest observers. After pausing briefly, it begins to retreat backward in the direction it came from. One almost expects to hear a long, soulful train whistle screaming in the night, and the throbbing, pounding *chugga-chugga* of an ancient locomotive engine that is

gathering speed. But the night is as still as death; the only pounding to be heard is the observer's racing heartbeat.

Finally, the light blinks off when it reaches its original starting point, leaving the startled viewers to wonder what, if anything, they really saw. After a few moments of silence, they begin to whisper quietly among themselves.

"Did you see what I saw?"

"I think so. What do you think it was? It couldn't have been a train, could it?"

"No, it wasn't a train. It was the ghost of old Joe Baldwin, swinging his lantern back and forth. He does it almost every night, all year round, in good weather or bad. They say he's looking for his head, and he'll keep on looking for it until he finds it."

At least, that's how the story goes. Thousands of people have seen the mysterious light. But no one has ever seen the ghost itself, although many people have tried.

Sometimes a brave individual walks along the tracks toward the light as it advances. When that happens, the light immediately blinks off and disappears. And whenever people have hidden themselves beside the tracks to the west of Maco Station in order to see the light at close range and find out what lurks behind it, the light simply has not appeared at all.

A viewer once was heard to exclaim in disgust, "Lookit them fools hidin' down there! Don't they know he won't show up again till they come back here? Joe Baldwin's momma didn't raise no fools!"

Stories about Joe Baldwin's headless ghost prowling the swampy area around Maco Station at night began sometime in the late 1800s. But are these stories really true? Does the departed conductor's restless spirit actually make nightly visits to the tracks? And does it carry his lantern in order to search for the head he lost in the fiery train wreck of 1867? As a lawyer would say, let's look at the facts.

First, there is the light itself. It is real, beyond any possible shadow of doubt. *Something* is causing the Maco Station Light to shine even today, more than a hundred years after it was first reported. We may disagree as to what causes the light to appear and disappear, but no one can argue that the light does not exist. Too many people—thousands upon thousands of eyewitnesses—have seen it for it to be some kind of illusion.

Even veteran railroad men have seen the light at Maco Station. In fact, so many railroad workers were fooled into thinking that a train was coming that the company ordered its signalmen to carry *two* lanterns at Maco Station, one red and one green.

Many people have tried to explain the light in realistic, unghostly terms, but so far no one has done so with any success.

The most common explanation given is that the light is due to automobile headlights. But the lights were first seen long before the automobile was invented, and before roads were built anywhere near the section of track where the light always appears.

Too, the lights are always seen on the railroad tracks, and usually they are seen by people who are standing on or very near the tracks. If a vehicle were "riding the rails" on its nightly visits, the eyewitnesses certainly would hear the sounds made by its engine as it sped toward and away from them. They would feel the vibrations of its wheels on the rails or roadbed. But no one has ever reported hearing any sounds or feeling any vibrations associated with the light that appears.

A second culprit that has been suggested as the cause of the Maco Station Light is swamp gas.

Sometimes strange lights can be seen moving over swamps or marshes at night. These lights, known as will-o'-the-wisps, are eerie, glowing gases produced by decaying animal or plant material.

The Maco Station area is swampy, all right—but if the light is nothing more than a glow produced by swamp gases, why does it disappear whenever anyone approaches it? And why does it regularly follow the same path, and the same precise routine, every time it is seen? Surely no one would suggest that swamp gas possesses intelligence, or that it has developed a system for eluding human observers who try to approach it!

All we know for sure about the Maco Station Light is that it exists. That, and the fact that it has resisted all attempts over the years to investigate its source or explain it as a natural phenomenon.

Maybe it *is* the restless spirit of conductor Joe Baldwin. If so, perhaps we can explain why his spirit can find no peace.

According to psychical theory, when a person dies suddenly in an unexpected or particularly violent manner, his spirit may not understand that he is no longer alive. And if, at the moment of death, his last conscious thoughts were that he had failed in some important task, his spirit may be filled with a powerful sense of guilt. As a result, it is unable to find peace in an afterlife beyond the grave. Unaware that it exists on a level somewhere beyond the land of the living, it endlessly repeats the person's last acts before death occurred.

In Joe Baldwin's case, his last act before dying was to wave his lantern frantically in an attempt to warn the oncoming train that the passenger cars were blocking its path. Some people say that, in death, his restless, guilt-filled spirit is *still* prowling the railroad tracks a short distance west of Maco Station.

He's not searching for his head, though—at least, not according to psychical theory. Instead, he is re-enacting the final moments of his life, trying to accomplish in death what he could not do in life. And until he succeeds, his ghostly light probably will continue to shine at night as it has done for nearly 120 years.

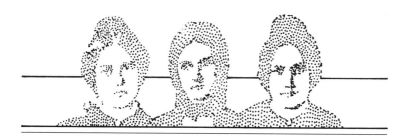

THE GIRLS WHO TALKED WITH THE DEAD

IF YOU DON'T BELIEVE IN GHOSTS, YOU PROBABLY WON'T BELIEVE THE story you're about to read. But before you leave this section and go on, perhaps you should take time to meet the Fox Sisters.

They were the first people ever to communicate with a ghost.

If you *do* believe in ghosts, you may be aware that they are thought to be the restless spirits of dead people who, for one reason or another, have not found peace beyond the grave. You may know, too, that there are thought to be two kinds of ghosts: apparitions and poltergeists. Apparitions are ghosts that are seen but not heard; poltergeists are heard but not seen.

Spiritualism is the belief that it is possible for living persons to reach beyond the boundaries of death and communicate with the spirits of the dead. The accepted method for achieving this is through a *seance*, a formal gathering of people who are trying to reach someone who is dead. At seances, messages are relayed to and from departed spirits through a *medium*, a person who is sensitive to messages from the spirit world.

The Spiritualist movement officially began on the night of March 31, 1848, in a small, run-down wooden cottage in Hydesville, New York. On that occasion two young girls, Kate and Margaret Fox, accidentally discovered their uncanny ability to cross the boundary line that separates the world of living persons from the realm of the dead.

The Poltergeist Appears · During the latter part of March, 1848, the poltergeist first made its presence known to the family of John Fox. One morning, strange rapping, knocking, and rattling sounds were heard in the house by the various family members, which included Mr. Fox, his wife, and their daughters Kate, Margaret, and Leah. (Another member of the Fox family was no longer living at home at the time: David, the girls' older brother, lived thirty miles away in Rochester.)

At first, the mysterious rapping noises did little more than upset the Foxes, who could find no cause for the disturbances. As days passed, though, the knocking sounds began to occur at all hours of the day and night. They grew in volume and intensity until the creaky old house seemed to be coming apart at the seams from the force of the pounding.

Leah, the oldest of the three Fox sisters, later wrote a book about the haunting. In it she said that at times the family had feared the roof would collapse on their heads from the violent pounding it seemed to be receiving. Neighbors reported hearing the disturbance from as much as a mile away: they said it sounded as if heavy artillery guns were being fired.

Then, on March 31, 1848, everything changed. And because of that night's shocking turn of events, humankind's relationship with the world of the supernatural took a giant leap forward. Since then, things have never been the same.

It was little seven-year-old Catherine, or Kate, who started the whole thing. She and her sister Margaret, aged ten, were in their bedroom listening to the noises. Suddenly, for no particular reason, Kate clapped her hands together. The pounding stopped, and in the empty silence that followed, both girls heard an answering clap. Kate snapped her fingers, and they heard a similar snapping sound.

Margaret decided to get into the act. She clapped, and then jumped in surprise when a clapping sound answered her. She ran to get her parents.

When John Fox arrived in his daughters' bedroom, they repeated their game for him, with the same results. He listened in stunned disbelief, and then tried it himself. No matter how many times he clapped his hands, the unseen force produced exactly the same number of claps.

The Foxes stared at each other in amazement. At this point, they had no idea who or what they were communicating with — but it was apparent that someone (or something) unseen was trying to communicate with them.

In the days that followed, the Foxes developed a system for communicating with the invisible force. They discovered that if, instead of clapping or snapping their fingers, they asked questions which could be answered by *yes* or *no*, the unseen presence would reply with one knock for *yes* and two knocks for *no*.

Using this simple code, they found that the presence in their house was the ghost of a man named Charles B. Rosmer. When alive, he had been a wandering peddler, and he had been murdered on the property and buried beneath the cottage. All this they learned by asking questions which the spirit could answer with *yes* (one rap) or *no* (two raps).

The Foxes began inviting neighbors in to hear their conversations with the ghost. And in a small town like Hydesville, it was not long before the ghost of Charles Rosmer was the talk of the town.

For several years before Mr. Fox had moved his family to

Hydesville from Canada, the cottage had been the scene of strange and unexplained noises. In fact, the previous tenant had left because the disturbances had unnerved and frightened him and his family. Now, a woman in the community came forward to tell her story.

Years before, she said, as a young girl she had been a maid for the family who occupied the cottage. One day a peddler arrived. He asked to spend the night with them, and the young maid was sent home. When she returned the following day, her employer told her that the peddler had already left. She had never thought of the incident again, she said, until she heard the ghostly rappings as the spirit tapped out answers which the Foxes had already learned but were replaying for their visitors' entertainment:

"Are you the ghost of Charles B. Rosmer?"

One tap. (*Yes.*)

"In life, were you a traveling salesman or peddler?"

One tap. (*Yes.*)

"Did you die a natural death?"

Two taps. (*No.*)

"Were you murdered?" (One tap.)

"Were you murdered on this property?" (One tap.)

"Are you buried here?" (One tap.)

Further questioning revealed that the body supposedly was buried beneath the cottage—at least, that was what the rappings indicated.

When the seance ended, Mr. Fox listened as the woman excitedly told her story. He decided to dig up the cellar and unearth the skeleton; after all, finding the man's remains would prove to anyone who doubted their story that no one in the Fox family had made it all up.

Unfortunately for the Foxes, he never found the skeleton. All the searchers found were a few bits and pieces of what may have been human bones buried beneath five feet of treated soil in the

cellar. No record ever was found of anyone named Charles Rosmer in the Hydesville area.

More than half a century later, though, in 1914, workmen digging on the property found a human skeleton buried near a wall beside the house. Among the bones was a tin box of the sort that peddlers used to keep their cash in.

News of this discovery, which appeared in leading newspapers of the day, led to the theory that the peddler probably had been buried *twice*: first in the cellar and then later in the yard by the wall. The murderer, whoever he was, may have feared that the corpse would be discovered someday if the house were torn down or rebuilt in the future.

In 1848, accounts of the strange goings-on in Hydesville, New York, spread quickly. All across the nation, people became fascinated with the idea that it might be possible to communicate with spirits of the dead. Mediums began cropping up like crabgrass in springtime. Supporters called their new movement "Spiritualism." And because the Fox sisters were the first people to achieve such communication, they quickly grew famous and were in great demand for public appearances. People everywhere, it seemed, wanted to see them perform.

Of course, not everyone believed in mediums and seances. Many people were convinced that Spiritualism was a hoax and the Fox sisters were frauds. But they willingly submitted to tests (such as standing on pillows or cushions with their ankles bound tightly together) in order to prove that they were not making the rapping sounds themselves. The sounds continued anyway, as if they were coming from the walls or the floor. No one was able to prove the charges of fraud.

Writing about the Fox sisters, famed editor Horace Greeley of the *New York Tribune* said, "We tested them [the sisters] thoroughly, and we were satisfied that they did not cause the 'rapping' sounds to be made."

Leah, eldest of the Fox sisters, was the first to become a professional medium. She began conducting seances for pay in the latter part of 1849. A few months later Kate and Margaret followed Leah's example; soon the sisters were touring America.

Gradually, the girls refined their seance methods. Instead of using the question-and-answer technique (one rap for *yes*, two raps for *no*), they began reciting the alphabet, with the spirit rapping at the proper letters. This allowed them to obtain direct quotes from their subjects in the spirit world.

At other seances the table would begin rocking on its legs, or else people would feel the touch of invisible hands. By 1860, Kate was reported to have produced visible spirit forms. She also produced spirit handwriting on blank cards while her hands were being held. A couple of times she even produced spirit voices.

In 1851, one of Margaret Fox's relatives published an article that said Margaret had confessed that she and her sisters were frauds. By this time, however, the Spiritualist movement was firmly established in the United States. It was growing so rapidly that little attention was paid to Margaret's alleged confession.

Later in the 1850s Margaret married and Leah married for a second time; both of them withdrew from public life. Kate, however, continued to give seances. She was hired as the personal medium for Charles Livermore, a wealthy New York banker. During the five years that Kate worked for Mr. Livermore, she gave nearly four hundred seances in his home, communicating with the spirit of his dead wife Estelle.

Eventually Margaret and Kate began having personal problems with Leah, who had returned to her work and established a highly successful career as a medium.

Possibly Margaret's resentment stemmed from the death of

her husband, which left her broke, unhappy, and in ill health. At any rate, Margaret and Leah argued frequently, and in May, 1888, Margaret publicly confessed that she and her sisters were frauds. Their seances, she wrote, had been "all fraud, hypocrisy and delusion." She arranged a lecture tour in which she exposed their methods: she showed audiences how she and Kate had learned to produce rapping sounds by snapping the joints of their fingers and toes.

A few months later, Kate also confessed and joined Margaret on the lecture tour. Perhaps they hoped to make money from their revelations; if so, they were sadly mistaken. Their tour failed to draw the large crowds they expected, and soon they gave up and went home. Margaret later took back her confession, saying that she had been emotionally upset and in financial trouble when she made her false admission of guilt.

Still, while the confessions of Kate and Margaret Fox created a scandal, they did not destroy the Spiritualist movement. By the time the sisters died—Leah, in 1890; Kate, in 1892; and Margaret, in 1893—Spiritualism was being practiced throughout the world.

And while the confessions of two of the Fox sisters tended to discredit all three of them, one haunting question remains unanswered: *If their communications with a ghostly spirit named Charles B. Rosmer were nothing more than a clever hoax, how did they know that a man had been buried on the property?* After all, his skeleton and tin money box were not unearthed until twenty-one years after the last of the Fox sisters died!

THE GREAT
AMHERST MYSTERY

IT WAS CALLED "THE GREAT AMHERST MYSTERY" AFTER A POPULAR
book of the same name which appeared in 1888.

Written by an American actor named Walter Hubbell, *The
Great Amherst Mystery* described the strange case of poltergeist
activity which affected the household of Daniel Teed and his
family in Amherst, Nova Scotia, during 1879 and 1880. The
drama centered around nineteen-year-old Esther Cox, who was
a younger sister of Mr. Teed's wife, and a devilish, fire-starting
ghost.

Amherst is a small town in the Canadian province of Nova
Scotia. It is located on the Bay of Fundy, where tides rushing in
from the Atlantic Ocean make the water level rise an average of
47½ feet with each high tide.

In 1879, Daniel Teed was thirty-five years old, the foreman of
a shoe factory. He lived in Amherst with his wife and large
family. In all, the Teed household consisted of eight persons:

Daniel and his wife Olive; their two sons—five-year-old Willie and one-year-old George; John Teed, who was Daniel's brother; Mrs. Teed's brother, William Cox; and Mrs. Teed's younger sisters, Jennie and Esther Cox. Jennie, aged twenty-two, was a beautiful and extremely popular young woman; Esther, nineteen, was less attractive than Jennie, and less outgoing in her manner. The Teed family lived together comfortably in a large, two-story yellow cottage.

The haunting began one night after everyone had gone to bed. Jennie and Esther were nearly asleep in their second-floor bedroom when suddenly Esther leaped out of bed with a cry of surprise and fright.

Jennie was instantly alert. Looking around in the darkness, she asked Esther what was wrong.

"There's a mouse under the covers!" Esther exclaimed.

Jennie lit her bedside lamp, and cautiously they searched the bed. There was no mouse among the bedcovers—but both of them saw straw moving inside the mattress.

"See?" Jenny said, pointing at the straw. "It has gone inside the mattress, and cannot find its way out. Let's go back to bed, Esther; it won't bother us again tonight." And with that the two girls returned to bed. They listened in the darkness for a few minutes for sounds of straw moving in the mattress, but heard nothing. Soon they drifted off to sleep.

The following night, both girls heard something moving under their bed. Assuming it to be the same bothersome mouse at work, the sisters climbed out of bed and lit their lamp. Jennie went to get a broom, and together they peeked under the bed, intending to kill the mouse if they found it. But the mouse wasn't there.

Instead, they found that the rustling noise was coming from a green cardboard box filled with scraps of cloth for patchwork. They slid the box out from under the bed and placed it in the middle of the floor. To their great surprise, the box and its contents jumped about a foot into the air, fell to the floor, and flopped over onto its side. Jennie dared to reach out and turn the box upright again. Once more it leaped into the air and landed with a loud clatter.

By now, the young women were thoroughly frightened. They screamed for Daniel (who, with his wife and sons, was asleep in the next room) to come and investigate the problem. He dressed hurriedly and rushed to their aid. They told him what had happened, but the box made no further movements in his presence.

Daniel emptied the box on the floor and found nothing but scraps of cloth inside. With a laugh, he replaced the scraps in the box, slid it back under the bed, told the girls that they must be crazy, and suggested that they return to bed.

The following morning, the sisters repeated their story to the entire family at breakfast, but no one believed them. At eight-thirty that night, Esther began to complain that she was not feeling well. Mrs. Teed suggested that she go to bed, which she did. Jennie joined her around ten o'clock.

Suddenly, at about ten-thirty, Esther shouted, "My God, what is the matter with me? I'm dying!" She leaped out of bed, taking the bedcovers with her. She stood, trembling, in the middle of the floor while Jennie lit a lamp.

Jennie stared at her sister in disbelief. Esther's face was blood-red, her eyes were bulging in their sockets, and her hair was standing almost straight out from her head. Jennie, not know-ing what to do for her poor sister, screamed as loudly as she could for the rest of the family to come to Esther's assistance.

Mrs. Teed arrived first, followed quickly by Daniel and John Teed and William Cox. They stared at Esther in amazement, thinking that she must be having some kind of fit. She appeared to be in terrible pain.

Suddenly, Esther grew pale and weak. She had to be helped

into bed. But then, seconds later, she leaped to her feet again, saying that she felt she was going to explode. Again she was led back to the bed where she lay in obvious misery.

"I am swelling up," she wailed, "and I shall certainly burst! I know I shall!"

She was indeed swelling, like a balloon being blown up. Her entire body was stretched and swollen out of shape, and she was screaming and writhing in pain.

But then, as the family watched in horror, they heard and felt the entire house being jarred by a loud, explosive *ker-whump*!

Mrs. Teed instantly was filled with fear for the safety of her young sons, who were asleep in another room. "The house has been struck by lightning!" she shouted. "My boys have been killed!" She and the three men rushed out of the bedroom to see to the boys' safety. But the children were sleeping peacefully, undisturbed by the strange goings-on around them.

Mrs. Teed glanced out the window. The sky was clear and cloudless above. The moon shone down brightly enough to cast shadows on the lawn. Olive Teed knew that, whatever the sound had been, it was not caused by a thunderclap or bolt of lightning.

The four adults returned to the sisters' bedroom and stood looking at Esther in horrified silence. She was still swollen far beyond her normal size, and she was crying and moaning loudly.

Then three more thunderous, explosive sounds rocked the house in rapid succession. They seemed to be coming from beneath the bed in which Esther lay. And with the unseen blasts, Esther's body returned to its normal size. She fell peacefully asleep.

Next morning, the family members agreed over breakfast not to tell anyone about the strange events of the previous evening. They suspected that no one would believe them anyway.

Four nights later, Esther suffered another swelling attack.

Again, Jennie summoned the others to Esther's bedside. Mrs. Teed restored Esther's bedcovers, which had been flung away to a distant corner of the room by some unknown force when the attack began.

No sooner had the covers been replaced than they flew off again to the same corner of the room. Then, at almost the same instant, the pillow beneath Esther's head sailed through the air and struck John Teed in the face. But Esther had not thrown the pillow. She was lying on her back with her arms at her sides.

"I've had enough of this," John said angrily. He turned and walked out of the room. The others remained at Esther's side, comforting her as best they could, until three more loud bangs shook the room. Esther's frightful swelling immediately went away, and again she drifted off into a deep sleep.

The following morning, Dr. Carritte, the family physician, laughed heartily when Daniel Teed told him what had happened in the Teed household during the past few days. He agreed to look in on Esther that evening, however, and said he would stay with her all night if necessary.

At ten o'clock, Dr. Carritte arrived. As he was examining Esther, her pillow shot out from under her head.

"Did you see that?" Dr. Carritte asked the others. They agreed that they had seen it too.

John Teed stepped close to Esther's side. "If it moves out again, it will not go back this time. I intend to hold on to it, even if it *did* bang me over the head last night."

As if by command, the pillow darted out from under Esther's head—except for one corner. John Teed took hold of the pillow, which was hanging suspended in midair, in order to keep it from flying back under Esther's head. But all of his strength, which was considerable, could not hold the pillow. It pulled away from him and returned to its former position beneath Esther's head.

Seconds later, three loud, banging sounds rang out from under the bed. Dr. Carritte searched beneath the bed, but found nothing that might have caused the explosive noises. As he stood up, the bedcovers flew off Esther and landed across the room. Then, as everyone watched and listened in silence, a new phenomenon occurred: the eerie, unmistakable sound of something scratching on the wall.

There, before their astonished eyes, a message began forming on the wall, as if it were being written by unseen hands with an invisible nail or other metal instrument.

Esther Cox, the message stated in large, poorly written letters, *you are mine to kill.*

A piece of plaster tore away from the wall, made a 90-degree turn in its flight, and landed at the doctor's feet. The room began to shake with violent, pounding sounds.

Dr. Carritte no longer was an unbeliever. He had no idea what kind of force was at work in the Teed household, but he had seen the handwriting forming on the wall. It was proof enough for him that some kind of mysterious power was making its presence known to them.

Next morning, Esther felt much better. She was helping Olive Teed with the housework when Dr. Carritte arrived. But when one of her chores sent her to the cellar, she soon came hurrying back upstairs complaining that someone had thrown a board at her.

Dr. Carritte went downstairs to investigate the matter. He searched the cellar thoroughly, but found neither the board nor anyone who might have thrown anything at Esther. He called to her to join him in the cellar, intending to show her that they were, in fact, alone. But as she joined him, potatoes began flying at their heads from a nearby potato bin until they retreated upstairs to safety.

That night, after the doctor looked in again on Esther, the

explosive sounds began anew. At first they were inside Esther's bedroom, but then they seemed to move onto the roof. Dr. Carritte went outside, where it sounded as if, in his words, "someone was on the roof with a sledgehammer, pounding and trying to break through the shingles." The night was bright and moonlit; Dr. Carritte could see that there was absolutely no one on the roof to produce the sounds.

When Dr. Carritte finally left around midnight, the sounds were still in progress. The doctor later said that the heavy, pounding noises could be heard as far away as two hundred yards from the house.

From that time on, the sounds began to occur throughout the day, beginning in the morning and continuing through the afternoon and evening. Passersby had no trouble hearing the loud disturbances; as a result, it was not long before the matter reached the attention of the Amherst *Gazette* and other local newspapers. Curious visitors began to show up regularly at the Teed cottage; they were eager to see and hear the mysterious, ghostly effects.

Among these visitors were several clergymen. One of them, the Rev. Dr. Edwin Clay, heard the sounds for himself and was convinced that neither Esther nor anyone else in the family was causing them. Another minister, the Rev. Dr. R. A. Temple, witnessed several events, including one occasion in which a bucket of cold water began to boil while it was resting on the kitchen table.

Then, in December, 1879, Esther came down with diphtheria. After recovering from her illness, she spent two blissfully uneventful weeks with an older, married sister in Sackville, New Brunswick. She went back to Amherst in high spirits, unaware that for her the worst was yet to come.

Not long after Esther returned, she and Jennie were in bed one night when a ghostly voice began to speak to her. She awakened her sister and told her what was happening.

"Ask it what it wants," Jennie suggested.

"He says that he was once alive, but now he's a ghost," Esther replied. "And he says that he's going to set fire to our house tonight!"

Jennie called in the other adults, and Esther repeated her story to them. The others laughed, because they knew there was no ghost. After all, there had been no further disturbances since Esther's return from New Brunswick. Besides, they argued, hadn't one of the ministers solved the mystery by blaming it on electricity that was coming from Esther's body?

Esther nodded slowly. Yes, she said, they were probably right. There was no ghost, there *couldn't* be—but the voice inside her head had seemed so *real*!

Suddenly, a lighted match dropped from the ceiling to the bed, in full view of everyone in the room. Jennie quickly put out the match before it could set the bed on fire.

During the next few minutes, ten more lighted matches materialized in the air and fell onto the bed or other areas of the room. Each time, someone quickly put out the flame. But then, before the startled eyes of the six witnesses in the room, a dress suddenly flew off a hook on the wall and landed on the floor. It rolled itself into a ball, slid under the bed, and burst into flames.

Daniel Teed was first to reach the burning dress. He jerked it out from under the bed and stamped out the flames with his boots.

Thus began a new kind of menace to the Teed household: the constant threat of fires started by the invisible ghost.

Three days after the ghost tried to set fire to Esther's bed, Olive Teed was busy at work in the kitchen. Esther was in the dining room with Jennie, where they had been working steadily for more than an hour. The two boys were playing outside in the yard, as they had been doing all morning.

Suddenly Mrs. Teed smelled smoke coming from the cellar. She cried out in alarm, grabbed a bucket of water in the kitchen, and raced downstairs. (After the events of the past few days, the Teeds kept water buckets available to deal with unexpected fires around the house.) She emptied her bucket onto a large pile of burning wood shavings whose flames threatened to spread to the timbers supporting the floor above. Then she and her younger sisters ran outside, screaming for help. Several neighbors quickly rushed in and doused the fire with water from the rain barrel outside. They smothered the remaining flames with rugs from the dining room.

By now, the odd goings-on at the Teed residence were no longer a local matter. Newspapers all over Canada carried headline stories about the case, fanning the flames of public interest with all sorts of theories about the disturbances and fires. By far, the most popular theory was the one advanced by the fire marshals of Amherst: they believed that Esther liked to set fires.

Daniel Teed knew the true story, of course. He and the others in the household, as well as Dr. Carritte, knew that Esther was an innocent victim of some evil force, just as *all* of them were. But in order to spare Esther's feelings, he decided to send her to live for a while with a Mr. and Mrs. White, who were close friends of the Teeds'. After all, he reasoned, the events had occurred only while Esther was in the house: during her two-week absence in December, there were no disturbances in the Teed household, and she had not suffered any swelling attacks.

Unfortunately, this time the ghost decided to follow her.

In less than a month's time, Esther was back at home. During her brief stay with the Whites, furniture had flown about as if flung by invisible hands — or worse, it had burst into flames and threatened to burn down the house. Mr. White said that, on one occasion, certain iron objects in Esther's lap "became too hot to be handled with comfort," and then they flew away from her to land in distant parts of the room. It was then that Mr. White decided that Esther was no longer welcome in his house.

Shortly after Esther returned home, a traveling band of actors came to town. One of the actors, Walter Hubbell, heard about the "haunted house" and decided to investigate it further. He talked at length with Daniel Teed and the others in the household about the haunting, and he even moved in with them for a while as a boarder.

Finding no evidence of fraud or hoax, Hubbell decided that the public would pay to see Esther and hear her incredible story. He convinced Mr. and Mrs. Teed to let him arrange a "lecture tour" featuring himself and Esther, with Mrs. Teed along as a chaperon for her younger sister.

The tour was doomed from the start. Audiences didn't want to hear Mr. Hubbell talk about Esther or ghosts: they wanted to *see* fires starting without any natural cause. And when Esther could not produce fires from thin air, they booed and threw things at the stage. Soon Mr. Hubbell admitted defeat and took Esther home.

When Esther came home, however, things quickly grew out of control. Mr. Hubbell barely was able to avoid a carving knife which flew straight at him from its resting place on a counter. On other occasions he found himself dodging an umbrella and a chair, and little George was constantly undressed in public by unseen hands.

Several times the ghost told Esther that it had started a fire somewhere in the house—but it would not tell her where. Several times it told her nothing at all, but merely waited for someone to discover the smoke or fire. At last, fed up with the goings-on and fearful for his property, the landlord who owned the house ordered Esther to be evicted. She could no longer live in the house with her family. She was sent to live with a Mr. and Mrs. Van Amburgh.

Not long after Esther moved in with the Van Amburghs, lighted matches materialized from nowhere, fell into a haystack, and burned down their barn. And because of the failed lecture tour, public sentiment favored the opinion that Esther was an arsonist, or fire-starter. She was taken to court, tried, and found guilty. She spent four months in jail.

Esther eventually married and raised a family of her own. And since no reports of further disturbances were reported either by Esther or by the family of Daniel Teed, we must assume that everyone lived happily ever after.

Was the Great Amherst Mystery a hoax? Dr. Walter F. Prince, writing in the *Proceedings* of the American Society for Psychical Research, stated that all of the disturbances were faked. But *why* should they have been faked?

After all, none of the family wanted to publicize the eerie goings-on; in fact, quite the opposite was true. As Walter Hubbell admitted, "They [the Teed family] concluded it was too deep a matter for them to talk about, and all agreed to keep it a secret and not inform any of their friends or neighbors what had transpired. They knew that no one would believe that such strange, unknown sounds [the explosions] had been heard under the bed, nor that Esther had been so singularly affected [by swelling] from unknown causes."

Does that sound like a family of tricksters who were searching for fame and fortune?

It was only when Walter Hubbell arrived and convinced the family that a "lecture tour" could prove financially profitable that they agreed to let Esther share her story with the public at large. And, more than anything else, it was the failure of the lecture tour that convinced the public that the Great Amherst Mystery was a hoax.

Esther's inability to start fires on command in public convinced the audiences that she was guilty of setting fires in the privacy of her home. People became convinced that she was a *pyromaniac*, or someone who cannot help but start fires just to watch things burn.

It is very easy to cry "Fake!" whenever anything out of the ordinary occurs. On the other hand, it must be admitted that clever tricksters can make ghosts and ghostly occurrences seem to appear.

But what often is ignored by those who cry "Fraud!" whenever supernatural events occur is that, almost without exception, they happen to ordinary people like *you* and *me*. People are going about their ordinary lives in their ordinary way when, all of a sudden, something extraordinary happens to them. And when it occurs, they are frightened or surprised by it—and they are not prepared to deal with it.

Whether it be a UFO sighting or the kind of ghostly misery inflicted upon the Teed household in the Great Amherst Mystery, the witness enters a world where telling others about his experience is likely to make him appear silly and foolish even among his best friends. But it does *not* necessarily make him a liar, a fraud, or a cheat.

After all, regardless of what anyone else says, his story may be true.

AN UNFINISHED
GHOST STORY

It was a warm, sunny afternoon in early autumn in South Georgia—the sort of day that was made for teenagers, swimsuits, and swimming holes. But none of the group of teenagers present that day in 1975 was thinking about swimming holes. Instead, they were listening intently to the woman who stood before them. She was telling a chilling ghost story, and no one wanted to miss a word of it.

Outside, a gentle breeze whispered its way through the towering oak tree in front of the house. Birds darted in and out among the huge limbs and thick, green foliage, whistling beneath a cloudless blue sky.

Inside the old, abandoned, two-story house known locally as the Cooper-Conner House, every eye in the assembled group of young people and adults was riveted on Mrs. Kitty Peterson. In addition to her other roles as wife, mother, journalist, author, and teacher, Kitty was also the best storyteller anyone ever

44

heard. Her favorite subject was ghost stories. And when Kitty told her ghost stories, it was said, even the ghosts stopped what they were doing and listened to her.

The group with Mrs. Peterson that afternoon consisted of students from Lyons Junior High School, along with a few parents and other chaperones. The students had looked forward to the trip with eager anticipation. Not only was it a chance to get away from school on a warm autumn afternoon, but Kitty's field trips were always fun. She had a way of making history come alive that later was to earn her honors as National History Teacher of the Year. Kitty had chosen the Cooper-Conner house for this particular trip because, more than anywhere else in Toombs or Montgomery Counties, it was tied up in the early history of the area.

Built sometime around 1821 by Major Richard Cooper, the house was designed to withstand raids by the Creek Indians who lived in the area at the time. Its outer walls consisted of huge pine timbers measuring sixteen inches wide and six inches thick. These massive, rectangular timbers were hand-cut, pinned together with two-inch wooden pegs, and dovetailed at the ends for a tight fit all around. They lend the house the appearance of a small fort, and with good reason: until recently Indian arrowheads still could be found imbedded in the outer walls of Cooper-Conner House.

The small motorcade of cars had passed through the city of Vidalia. Then, still heading west, it entered the Dead River area and stopped at the Dead River Cemetery. There, Kitty showed the students the graves of Major Cooper and two other members of the Georgia Militia who fought in the Revolutionary War. (One of those men was Captain Wilson Conner, who later entered the ministry and became a well-known circuit preacher. He acquired the house after Major Cooper's death in 1863. That's why it's called the Cooper-Conner House.)

Later, Kitty led the group of cars off the highway a few hundred yards beyond the cemetery. They turned left onto a narrow, overgrown, one-lane dirt road that wound its way through a dense pine forest. Then, after traveling a half mile along the bumpy, rutted trail through the woods, the cars halted again. After eating their bag lunches, everyone set out on foot for the house. As they walked, Mrs. Peterson warned them to watch out for poison ivy and snakes. Some of the rattlers in the area are as thick as a man's forearm.

At the house, Kitty explained that certain changes had been made over the years since 1821. The outer foundation blocks eventually rotted and were replaced with concrete blocks. The roof, which originally consisted of planks covered by split boards, was now covered with sheets of tin. And inside, the brick fireplaces at either end of the house had fallen into a state of disrepair and had been repaired with new bricks. Virtually everything else was as it was 150 years ago when the house was built.

Having said those things, Kitty let the students look around downstairs for a while. Then she led them up the steep, narrow staircase to the second floor.

Mrs. Peterson's ghost story that afternoon had nothing to do with the Cooper-Conner house. Instead, it told of a salesman who, needing shelter one stormy night, came upon a dark, forbidding house in the woods. He was told by the owner of the house—a tall, powerfully built man with fierce, glaring eyes and a hatchet in his hand—that he could sleep in the attic if he was willing to pay the price.

"And what price is that?" the salesman asked.

The man grinned cruelly. "You'll find out." Before the salesman could reply, the man pointed to the barn.

"You can leave your horse and wagon in there," he growled, and slammed the door in the salesman's face.

For a moment the salesman considered leaving. But night was fast approaching, and the wind was picking up. Every few seconds, the darkening sky blazed with lightning. Thunder began to roll, bringing with it the first raindrops of a summer rainstorm . . .

. . . And at that point in Kitty's story, the skies grew dark outside the Cooper-Conner house. Everyone in the room plainly heard the rumbling thunder of a real rainstorm approaching.

Kitty, who was standing by one of the four upstairs windows and facing her audience, recalls thinking, *I'd better send one of the boys downstairs to close the car windows.* But when she turned to look outside, she found that though the sky was dark, it was perfectly clear. A soft breeze was coming from the direction of the front of the house.

Kitty went to the other side of the house and looked out those windows, too, but there was not a single cloud to be seen anywhere. The sky had turned the same deep blue color as the ocean, and for no apparent reason. It was not yet two o'clock in the afternoon.

Some of the adults in the group wanted to leave before the sandy road turned muddy in the rain—but there was no rain, and no rainclouds. The students urged Kitty to finish her story.

The attic in Kitty's ghost story was reached via a trap door and ladder. The owner of the house went first, Kitty said. He climbed the ladder and pushed the hinged trapdoor up and out of the way. Then he climbed back down, stepped aside, and made an upward motion with his arm.

"Go ahead," he snarled. "There's a bed up there. It ain't much, but it's good enough for the likes of *you!*"

The salesman meekly climbed the ladder and entered the attic. All he carried with him was a small bag containing his money and a few personal items. The rest of his belongings were in his wagon in the barn.

Although the salesman was a small man, he could not stand fully erect in the attic: there was less than five feet of clearance between the roof and the floor. He laid his bag aside and rose, still bent forward from the waist. He glanced around, squinting as he tried to accustom his eyes to the darkness.

The owner's head and shoulders appeared in the opening at the top of the ladder. He set his lantern down on the floor beside him but did not enter the attic. In its yellow glow the details of the room became visible.

"The bed's over there," the man grunted, pointing.

The salesman turned and saw the bed, fifteen feet away from where he stood. It lay against a wall, beneath a small, barred window. There was a shape on the bed—a human shape. It was a man, and from fifteen feet away he appeared to be asleep. In the lantern's glow the man's features were vaguely familiar.

The salesman walked over to the edge of the bed. He had to lean forward as he went to avoid bumping his head on the overhead beams. Still leaning over, he stared at the man. He was lying on his back with his eyes closed. He was covered by a blanket up to his chin.

Suddenly, the salesman's eyes widened in recognition. "I think I know this man!" he whispered loudly. "What's he doing up here, anyway? He's—"

"Yeah," the man on the ladder said coldly, picking up his lantern. "He's dead. Just like *you're* gonna be before long." He quickly reached for the handle of the trapdoor, swung it shut above him, and . . .

. . . Just then everyone listening to Kitty's story jumped in sudden fright. Downstairs, the front door had slammed shut with a thunderous crash that shook the house, solid as it was.

Kitty calmly asked one of the students to go and see if anyone else was in the house with them. When he returned a couple of minutes later, he was laughing nervously, trying not to appear frightened.

"Nobody's there," he said. "I looked around, but there wasn't anybody else inside or outside the house. But—didn't we hear the door slam shut?" Heads nodded in agreement.

"It must have been the wind that blew it closed," someone suggested.

The boy shook his head and sat down with the others. "Uh-uh. When I went downstairs, the door was standing wide open. And the wind—" He hesitated.

"What about the wind?" Kitty asked.

"Well, there's not much wind outside, just a breeze," he said, pointing to the window behind Kitty. "But it's blowing the wrong way to have closed the door. The wind would have *opened* the door, not closed it."

"Maybe the wind blew it closed and then opened it again," someone suggested. The remark drew a few nervous giggles from the students, but Kitty shook her head. She knew that it would take more than a gentle breeze to open or close the heavy front door of Cooper-Conner House.

"Then what made the crash we heard?" a girl asked. "Could something heavy have fallen onto the floor?"

The boy shook his head. "No way. The house is empty downstairs, same as it is up here. There's nothing down there to fall, except the ceiling—and that's the floor that we're sitting on. Did anybody notice the floor collapsing up here?"

"What do *you* think, Mrs. Peterson?" the girl asked.

"I think somebody's playing a trick on us," Kitty replied. But a hasty count of heads revealed that everyone was present and accounted for. Kitty, who was facing the others as she told her story, says that, except for the boy she sent downstairs, no one left or re-entered the room while she was talking.

"Aw, it was just a ghost, that's all," a student said. "Go ahead and finish the story you were telling us, Mrs. Peterson. What happened to the salesman in the attic?"

Kitty glanced around the group. Other students chimed in, urging her to finish her ghost story. They still had no idea that they were involved in a ghost story themselves.

After closing the trapdoor to the attic, Kitty said, the man quickly slid the heavy bolt into place. The salesman could hear him laughing coarsely as he climbed down the ladder. His heavy boots thudded loudly with each step he took.

Lightning flashed, spreading light momentarily through the attic. The salesman dropped to his hands and knees and crawled over to the trapdoor. He banged on it, hammered at it with both fists, and pleaded with the man to let him out, but to no avail. The man's only response was harsh, scornful laughter.

Finally, the salesman gave up and sat back on his heels. He knew that he had to control the rising tide of panic within him. He was alone in the darkness—alone, that is, except for the corpse lying on the bed. It was, he suspected, another salesman in the area who had been reported missing recently.

The salesman fumbled around in the darkness until he located his bag on the floor. But there was nothing in the bag he could use to help him escape from the attic, nothing with which he might defend himself against the man with the hatchet.

He was trapped, helpless, like an insect in a jar.

Suddenly, he heard a strange noise—a high-pitched, rasping sound. He gasped in surprise, thinking that the corpse on the bed might be coming back to life. In the darkness he could picture the corpse sitting up in bed and wheezing as it forced air in and out of useless, dead lungs. But the sound seemed to be coming from downstairs.

The salesman noticed a small circle of light to his left as the grinding sound went on. It was a knothole, a hole in the attic floor. He knelt down and put his eye to the hole.

The owner of the house was sitting in front of a large grinding wheel. His feet were pumping up and down, turning a series of belts and cog wheels which turned the grinding stone.

The man was sharpening his hatchet blade.

Every few seconds he paused to test the sharpness of the blade against his forearm. Finally, when he drew a small trickle of blood, he rose and stepped away from the wheel. He glanced up toward the attic and grinned: it was the kind of evil grin that a hungry spider might give to flies caught in its web. He was looking directly at the knothole when he spoke.

"Soon, little man," he said in a harsh, icy voice. "Very soon now. I haven't forgotten about you. But I have work to do. And you might want to see to your friend. For all I know, he has a gun with him under the blanket." Then he began to laugh again, a deep, rumbling laugh that mingled with the rolling thunder outside.

The salesman sat up and backed away from the knothole. He was sweating now, and his heart was pounding wildly as he tried to collect his thoughts.

He had to get out of there! The man was *crazy*! What he needed was a weapon of some kind—a knife or a gun . . . Wait a minute! What if there really *was* a gun under the blanket? Or better yet, what if the man on the bed wasn't really dead? After all, the madman downstairs might have lied to him about the man's being dead. Maybe he was just a sound sleeper. If so, they might not need a gun at all. He could rouse the man from his sleep, and together they could set a trap for the maniac with the hatchet. When he came upstairs, they could attack him from both sides and disarm him. And maybe they'd leave *him* locked in the attic when they left tomorrow!

The salesman scrambled across the floor on his hands and knees. He was excited about his plan. Now, all he had to do was awaken his sleeping roommate.

He climbed onto the bed and crawled to where the man's head lay. Kneeling, he reached out and took hold of the man's shoulders.

"C'mon, Fred," he whispered urgently, shaking the man's shoulders gently. "Wake up. We've got to—"

He never finished his sentence. At that moment, a lightning bolt blasted the skies outside with a jarring crash and dazzling burst of white light. And in that moment of illumination, the man's head fell off.

The salesman screamed as the head rolled away from the shoulders it had rested upon. It rolled down the pillow, onto the bed, and into the salesman's lap. He screamed again and pushed the grisly object away from him.

And then, to complete the horror, the salesman heard a deep voice calling out to him from below, "I'm comin' for you now, little man! Get ready: it's time for you to die, just like your friend up there!"

The salesman began to tremble uncontrollably. He wanted to escape, or to hide somewhere—but there was no way out, nowhere to hide. So he sat, shivering and quaking in fear on the bed, listening to the heavy *step step* of the feet climbing slowly up the ladder to the attic . . .

. . . And at that moment everyone who was listening to Kitty Peterson's ghost story heard the unmistakable sound of footsteps advancing slowly, in rhythmic fashion, up the steep, narrow stairs of Cooper-Conner House. It wasn't human footsteps that they heard, though; everyone who was there that day agrees that the sharp, clacking noises sounded like some kind of hoofed animal climbing the staircase.

Eyes widened in alarm, and heads turned nervously to see what kind of animal would appear at the top of the stairwell. (Kitty and most of the others thought it sounded like a deer on the stairs.) But no animal appeared.

The room grew deathly quiet. Students and adults alike turned to each other with unbelieving expressions on their faces, silently asking their neighbors, *Do you hear what I hear?* The hoof-like footsteps continued on the stairs.

It was Kitty who finally broke the spell. She called two of the students by name and asked them to see what was making the noise. They nodded, rose from their sitting positions on the floor, walked across the room, and peeked around the corner of the stairwell.

"There's nothing there!" the boy announced loudly. The girl who was with him nodded in agreement.

"Are you sure?" someone asked.

"Maybe it went downstairs," someone else suggested. Several others nodded. Kitty asked the two students if they would mind looking around downstairs. They did so, and returned shortly.

"Nothing," the boy said, shaking his head. "But the front door is closed now. If it went downstairs it must have jumped out of one of the windows."

Another student spoke up. Like several of the boys in the group, he was an avid hunter. "Let's go see if we can find tracks outside."

That seemed a very good suggestion to most of the group. They made their way down the narrow stairs in single file, and reassembled on the front porch. Most of them were relieved to be outside again. This definitely had *not* been the kind of field trip that anyone had expected!

The students had no trouble finding tracks in the weeds and sandy soil outside the house. The entire yard was literally

covered with hoofprints that circled the house. But while deer tracks were not at all uncommon in Toombs and Montgomery Counties, the teenage hunters in the group seemed to think that these hoofmarks were made by a ram, not a deer.

Finally, Mrs. Peterson suggested that it was time for them to go. When no one offered any serious objections to her suggestion, they began walking back to their cars.

They had not gone very far when one of the boys who was leading the way stopped. He had noticed something very unusual.

"Look!" he said excitedly, pointing at the ground.

"So what?" one of the girls replied. "It's just some more hoofprints like the ones we saw in the yard, and the footprints we made when we came. See? There aren't any footprints ahead of us going the other way, because we haven't been that way yet."

"Yeah," the boy replied, "but the hoofprints are on top of our footprints. Whatever made those tracks, made them *after* we came."

And that was the end of the mysterious affair at Cooper-Conner House—or so Kitty Peterson thought.

Another eighteen months passed before Kitty found out exactly what she and her students had encountered: the ghostly curse that had been laid on Cooper-Conner House.

The house had been built by Major Richard Cooper, an officer in the American colonies' war for independence from England.

Major Cooper was fiercely loyal to the colonists' cause. As a result, he had nothing but contempt for Tories—the people living in America who wanted the colonies to remain in English hands.

The major's wartime duties required him to visit Savannah frequently. On one of his trips there, he met a Tory and the two men quickly developed a bitter hatred for each other. Their mutual hatred soon grew into a full-scale feud: each man vowed that he would not rest until he had killed the other.

Finally, the feud came to a head when the two men happened to meet in a tavern in Savannah. Loud, angry words soon led to a bloody brawl, and in that fight Major Cooper shot and killed the Tory.

As he lay mortally wounded on the tavern floor, the Tory fixed his gaze on Major Cooper. His eyes were bright with pain and hatred.

"You haven't heard the last of me," he grunted. "I'm not . . . finished with you yet, Major Cooper!" And then he died.

Shortly after the major returned to his home in Montgomery County, his servants began to complain that strange things were going on in the house. Doors that had been locked securely at night were found standing wide open the next morning, or else they were heard slamming shut with a resounding bang when they had been bolted previously. Servants and family members alike often heard the sounds of animal hoofs walking across empty floors or climbing the steep, almost vertical stairway to the second floor.

No one ever was injured by the Tory's ghost—if indeed that's what was responsible for the ghostly occurrences in Major Cooper's House. But over the years the story of the ghost ram was passed along from generation to generation of owners until it became an accepted part of the private history of Cooper-Conner House.

At first reading, this story may appear to be nothing more than a simple ghost story—a legend passed on by the owners of Cooper-Conner House. But as is true of most ghost stories taken from real life, this one has a catch to it that cannot easily be explained away as fiction. It is this:

At the time of Mrs. Peterson's field trip to Cooper-Conner House in the fall of 1975, *neither she nor anyone else who went along with her knew that the house was haunted.* They knew nothing of the dying Tory's last words, or of a ghost ram that was said to prowl the house and property, searching for descendants of its bitter enemy, Major Cooper. All Kitty or the others knew was that Cooper-Conner House was the oldest house still standing in Montgomery or Toombs Counties, and that it had been designed to withstand Indian attacks.

It was not until much later, in the spring of 1977, that Kitty finally learned that a true ghost story was associated with the house. She learned about it through a historical paper supplied to the Vidalia Public Library by Mrs. Anice McArthur, who is married to a distant descendant of the Rev. Wilson Conner who acquired the house after Major Cooper died.

In her paper, which sketched the history of Cooper-Conner House from its construction in 1821, Mrs. McArthur included a section dealing with Major Conner's feud with the Tory, and she wrote about the story of the ghost ram as well.

When Kitty Peterson read about the ghost ram, she understood what she and her students had heard that day back in 1975. They had heard the echoes of a dying man's promise to return in some form from beyond the grave: "I'm not . . . finished with you yet, Major Cooper!"

As for the ghost story that Mrs. Peterson was telling her students when she was interrupted by the sounds of hoofs on the stairs—well, it's still unfinished. She never told them the rest of the story.

She says, though, that she'll be glad to finish it for us. But first, she wants us to take a trip with her—a short trip, really, only fifteen miles out in the country from downtown Vidalia. After stopping by to get the key from Don McArthur, who owns the house and property, we'll turn off the highway just past the Dead River Cemetery. Then, Kitty says, all we have to do is follow the overgrown dirt road that leads through the woods to Cooper-Conner House . . .

Strange
Appearances
and Disappearances

THE BOY
FROM NOWHERE

SHOEMAKER GEORGE WEICHMAN LOOKED UP WHEN THE BOY EN-tered his shop. The place was Nuremberg, Germany; the date, May 26, 1828.

Weichman stared at the boy. Never in all his years had he seen such a strange sight.

The boy appeared to be sixteen or seventeen years old. His hair was long and dirty. He was wearing ill-fitting, peasant's clothes, and he seemed to have great difficulty walking. He squinted and blinked constantly, as if the bright sunlight outside hurt his eyes.

"Yes? What is it?" the shoemaker asked. The boy did not reply. His nervous manner indicated that he was confused and afraid.

"Are you lost, boy?" Weichman asked. Still the boy said nothing. He appeared unsteady on his feet, and the shoemaker wondered if the boy was either drunk or retarded.

At last the boy cleared his throat. "I—I-want-to-be-a-soldier-like-my-father-was," he said in a robotlike voice. He reached into his pocket and produced a handwritten note. He gave it to Weichman, who read it carefully.

The note was unsigned, but it appeared to have been written by a man. He said that the boy had been left on his doorstep in 1812. He had ten children of his own, he said, and he had not let the boy out of his house for sixteen years. Now he asked that the boy be taken into the German army. Either that, the note said, or "If you do not want him, you can kill him."

The shoemaker looked up at the boy. "Who are you?" he asked. Again the boy did not answer him.

Thinking that the boy might be hungry, Weichman offered him meat, bread, and milk. The boy gobbled down the bread as if he had not eaten in a long time. He also drank some water, but he acted as if he had never seen milk or meat before.

When the boy had finished eating, Weichman took him to the police station. There, the boy pointed to his chest and said, "Kaspar-Hauser." Then he repeated his singsong statement that he wanted to be a soldier as his father had been. The policemen questioned Kaspar thoroughly, but his only other reply was a dull "I-don't-know." They concluded that he must be retarded.

What they didn't know at the time was that those few words in German were virtually the only ones that Kaspar knew.

The policemen found a second note in Kaspar's clothes. It was also handwritten. This time the writer claimed to be his mother. She said that his name was Kaspar and he had been baptized; his father, an ex-soldier, was dead; and she was too poor to take care of Kaspar. The officers concluded that both notes were fake. But Kaspar could not have written them: he didn't know how to write.

One of the policemen took Kaspar home with him. Before long, he discovered exactly how strange a boy Kaspar Hauser was.

At first, when Kaspar walked he looked like a baby taking its first awkward steps. He stumbled over objects in his path rather than walking around them. The soles of his feet were tender and thin-skinned, indicating that he had never walked much, if at all.

Other aspects of Kaspar's behavior were equally unusual and mysterious.

When he entered the policeman's house for the first time, he tried to grasp the flame of a candle apparently because he thought it was pretty. It burned his hand. He was frightened by moonlight and loud noises. And during his first few days in the policeman's house, foods other than bread and water made him sick.

Kaspar's vision was perfect, but he seemed to be severely colorblind—as if he had spent much of his life in darkness. Indeed, bright lights hurt his eyes, and he could see in the dark like an animal. His sense of smell was much keener than the average human's. Strangest of all, Kaspar could even see stars in the sky during the daytime as well as at night.

As word of the strange boy began to spread throughout Germany, he attracted the attention of a Professor Daumer who agreed to work with Kaspar. He began teaching Kaspar, and found him to be intelligent and a quick learner. Soon, Kaspar was able to tell the professor what his earlier life had been like. And like practically everything else about the boy, his story was astonishing.

Before his arrival in Nuremberg (Kaspar said), he spent his entire life in a small cell that was six or seven feet long, four feet wide, and no more than five feet high. His only companion was a wooden toy soldier. He slept on a bed of straw in his unlighted cell, and he never had seen another human until the day a man brought him to Nuremberg.

Each morning when he awoke, he found fresh bread and water in his cell. Sometimes, the water tasted bad and he fell asleep after drinking it. When he awoke, he'd find that he had been washed, his hair and nails trimmed, and his cell cleaned while he was asleep.

One day, Kaspar said, a man entered his cell. The man taught him to say a few words—"Kaspar Hauser," "I don't know," and "I want to be a soldier like my father was"—and carried him outside his underground cell for the first time in his life. The bright sunlight made him dizzy, and he fainted. When he awoke, he was lying outside the shoemaker's shop in Nuremberg.

Meanwhile, the police were still trying to find out who the boy named "Kaspar Hauser" really was. Posters bearing his likeness were spread throughout Germany and the rest of Europe with little success. Everyone was interested in the case, but no one seemed to know anything about the boy.

A man came forward to announce that he had found a bottle with a message inside it. The note was a plea for help from someone who said he was being held prisoner in a cell on the banks of the Rhine River. The note was signed *Hares Sprauka* which, the police noted, was "Kaspar Hauser" with the letters rearranged. But Kaspar said that he had written no such note— in all his years living in a cell, he didn't know that he was a prisoner because he had no idea what life was like outside the cell. Besides, he pointed out, he didn't even know how to write at the time.

The police made a thorough search along the banks of the Rhine, but they found no such prisoner or cell.

In October, 1829, Kaspar was attacked and left unconscious and bleeding in the policeman's home by a man wielding a club. Kaspar did not see his attacker's face, and he had no idea why he was assaulted.

The man, who had worn a mask, was never identified or caught. All the police knew for sure was that the man had not been a burglar: except for the cellar where Kaspar was attacked, the house was undisturbed. No money, jewelry, silverware, or other valuables were missing.

During the next four years, Kaspar lived with several different guardians. The last of his guardians was an Englishman, Lord Charles Stanhope. Lord Stanhope took Kaspar to live in his home in Ansbach, Bavaria.

On December 14, 1833, Kaspar received a note asking him to meet someone in a public park in Ansbach. If he did so, the note explained, he would find out who his mother and father were.

At the park, Kaspar met a man he later described as having a thick beard and moustache and wearing a long, dark coat.

"Are you Kaspar Hauser?" the man asked. Kaspar replied that he was. The man offered him a purse, but as he accepted it the man stabbed him in his side and ran away. The wound was severe, but Kaspar somehow managed to get home before he collapsed, bleeding and in shock. He died three days later.

The police investigated the case. They found the purse lying in the snow, but no murder weapon was ever found. They discovered, too, that the only footprints leading to and from the purse belonged to Kaspar Hauser. But before he died, Kaspar told the police that he had not stabbed himself. He could not identify his attacker.

Kaspar was buried in Ansbach cemetery. On the tombstone over his grave are these words: "Here lies Kaspar Hauser, an enigma of his time, of unknown birth, of peculiar death, 1833."

Was Kaspar Hauser Telling The Truth? · Even if we would like to believe Kaspar Hauser's weird tale of being imprisoned alone in a tiny cell as far back as he could remember, his story does not ring true. It just doesn't *sound* right. After all, is it possible that he never once saw another human being before the man suddenly appeared one day to teach him a few words and take him to Nuremberg?

Kaspar was sixteen or seventeen years old when he showed up at the shoemaker's shop. He must have undergone periods of illness in his earlier years: times when he needed medical or dental treatment, or times when he ran a high fever and needed constant, close attention. How could he have received such treatment without at least once accidentally seeing someone? Even if we assume that he was given knock-out drugs in his food whenever other humans needed to approach him, he could not have survived being given such powerful drugs when he was running a high fever.

Other questions are equally baffling. For instance, how was his cell heated and cooled? He said that his cell was located deep underground; if it was not heated or cooled to allow for changes in the seasons, he must have been sick much of the time, which leads us back to the previous questions about his health. And if his cell was artificially heated, he could not have failed to see someone adjusting the heat in some manner during his sixteen years of confinement.

Finally, if, as he said, he had been deprived of contact with other humans all his life, he should have been severely unstable emotionally. Studies involving animals who are kept away from other animals from birth have shown that they quickly develop signs of extreme mental illness. Even when they are allowed to mingle with other animals later, they never overcome the mental problems that developed early in their lives. Yet no such evidence exists that Kaspar Hauser was mentally ill or unable to live a normal life around other people.

On the other hand, why would he lie about his past? And more importantly, *could* he have lied about it? It seems hardly possible that he could have faked all of his physical problems and talents—inability to walk, seeing in the dark, sunlight hurting his eyes, his keen sense of smell, throwing up whenever he had food other than bread and water, and so forth.

But even these problems seem unimportant when compared to the most important question of all.

Where Did Kaspar Hauser Come From? • No one ever found out where the boy came from. He showed up one day in May, 1828; he was stabbed to death in December, 1833. And to this day, his true origin is still a mystery.

The story of Kaspar Hauser was well-known throughout Europe. Several theories were offered as to his true identity and where he came from.

According to one such theory, Kaspar was the secret son of an innkeeper's daughter and a priest. Another theory had him coming to earth from another planet, set down among us so the alien creatures could study the way humans reacted to him.

By far the most popular theory at the time was that Kaspar was the son of Grand Duke Karl Frederick and Grand Duchess Stephanie, the ruling family of Baden.

Immediately after his birth (or so the rumor went), Kaspar was kidnapped and taken from the Duke's palace. He was replaced by a dead baby. (The duke had no children; without a direct heir his throne would pass to another branch of his family when he died.) Meanwhile, young Kaspar secretly was taken to live with an ex-soldier who was in league with the kidnappers. Years later, when the boy grew too large to remain in the cell (or when the ex-soldier grew tired of keeping him), the world got its first glimpse of Kaspar Hauser.

And if you accept this latter version of Kaspar's origin, you'll probably decide that the two attempts to kill him were made because he was the rightful heir to the throne of Baden.

You may be right, too.

Kaspar Hauser was said to bear a strong resemblance to the duke and duchess. If so, he may have been murdered because his continued existence was seen as a threat to the man who succeeded to the throne when the grand duke died in 1830. (It is interesting that the Earl of Stanhope—Kaspar's final legal guardian who took him to live in Ansbach, Bavaria, where he was murdered in 1833—was a close friend of the man who eventually inherited the throne.)

But we'll probably never know for sure who Kaspar Hauser really was, or why he was murdered. And that's why even now, more than 150 years after his mysterious life and death, the story of Kaspar Hauser remains one of the most fascinating unexplained mysteries in Europe's long and colorful history.

THE LOST COLONY

W<small>HAT HAS BEEN CALLED THE FIRST AND OLDEST MYSTERY IN</small> A<small>MERI</small>-can history began innocently enough on April 27, 1584.

On that date, Sir Walter Raleigh set sail from England, heading west across the Atlantic Ocean and bound for North America. He had two ships filled with men, weapons, food, and supplies. His goal was to explore and claim land in the New World for England and Queen Elizabeth I.

Sir Walter Raleigh landed at Roanoke Island on July 13, 1584. After exploring the area, which lies along the coast of North Carolina, he returned to England to tell the queen of his discovery. She was greatly pleased.

At that time, England was involved in a race with France, Spain, and Portugal to lay claim to the rich lands of the New World that Christopher Columbus had discovered nearly a century earlier. In the 1500s, Spain and Portugal had grown wealthy by shipping countless tons of gold from Central and South America back to Europe; England wanted to gather her share of treasures, too—but even more important, she needed natural resources such as lumber and iron for building boats. America possessed both in great quantities.

Still, it was one thing to lay claim to new and unexplored territories; it was another thing altogether to protect the settlers and colonists from the Indians and other nations who wanted the land for themselves.

The following spring, Raleigh sent seven more ships loaded with colonists—108 persons in all—to organize a settlement on Roanoke Island. They reached the island on July 27, 1585. The settlers quickly cleared land for farming and made homes for themselves. They also built a small fort on the island for protection.

The fort soon proved useful. As the result of a dispute between the settlers and Indians living in the area, the colonists burned an entire Indian village to the ground. After that, a virtual state of war existed between the two groups.

The settlers clearly were at a disadvantage; they needed supplies from England such as weapons and ammunition, but England could not offer them much aid. All available British ships were fighting against the powerful Spanish armada, or fleet, that was threatening England.

The colonists soon grew desperate. Surrounded by unfriendly Indians, they could no longer farm the land outside the fort to provide food for themselves. They were running low on ammunition, too, and the expected supply ship from England was long overdue. It would be just a matter of time before they were overwhelmed by the Indians.

Finally, in June, 1586, the British sea captain Sir Francis Drake arrived with armed soldiers and a fleet of twenty-three ships. He explained the situation to the settlers and offered to take them back to England. They did not want to go, but reluctantly they accepted his offer. Drake left fifteen soldiers on Roanoke Island to protect the colony for the Queen, gave them enough supplies and arms to last for two years, and returned to England with the colonists.

But when the overdue supply ship arrived sometime later in that year, all the captain and crew found on Roanoke Island was a deserted settlement.

In 1587, Sir Walter Raleigh organized a second expedition to Roanoke Island. Under the leadership of Governor John White, more than one hundred colonists set out for their new home in America.

When they arrived at Roanoke Island, they found that the original fort had been destroyed and the soldiers were gone, apparently killed by Indians. They rebuilt the fort, restored old houses and built new ones, and fought with the Indians. And on August 18, 1587, a baby girl, Virginia Dare, was born on Roanoke Island. The granddaughter of Governor White, she was the first white person ever born on American soil.

Nine days after Virginia Dare was born, her father and grandfather joined a crew of fifteen men who sailed back to England for additional supplies that would be needed by the colonists in the winter months ahead. Before Governor White departed in the only available ship, he left careful instructions for the remaining colonists. If, for any reason, they were forced to abandon the settlement at Roanoke Island, they should leave specific information regarding their whereabouts "in a conspicuous place." Lacking time for such a message of distress, they were to leave the sign of a Maltese cross ✠ prominently displayed somewhere in the area.

With those instructions, the governor and his crew departed for England on August 27, 1587. England was now openly at war with Spain for control of the seas, and as a result three long years would pass before the governor was able to return to Roanoke Island. In his absence, a mystery would arise which has never been fully solved. Perhaps it never will be. It is the baffling mystery of the Lost Colony of Roanoke Island.

On August 17, 1590, Governor White finally stepped ashore on Roanoke Island after an absence of three years. He was eager to find out how his wife, daughter, granddaughter, and the other colonists had fared while he was gone. But no one came to greet the ship, and no one answered the calls of Governor White or the sailors with him. The silence was as deep and complete as the inside of a tomb.

Hurrying to the settlement, the men found a disturbing scene before them.

There was no trace of the more than one hundred colonists who had been left behind to defend the tiny settlement. Some of the houses had been torn down, while others were still standing but abandoned. The fort still stood, but there were no bodies or skeletons lying around to indicate that a battle had taken place. The entire area was overgrown with weeds and tall grass; obviously, no one had lived there for a long time.

The men were baffled. Where had everyone gone? Had they been attacked by Indians and forced to abandon their settlement? If so, why hadn't they left a message as Governor White had instructed them to do? And if not, why would they permanently abandon the safety of their fort? And how could a colony of at least 115 persons vanish from the face of the earth?

As the men argued these questions among themselves, one of them found the clue they had been looking for. "Over here!" he called to the others. "I think I've found something!"

And so he had.

Carved into a tree trunk near the fort was a single word: CROATOAN.

That one word, carved into the trunk of a tree, was the only real clue ever unearthed as to the fate of the missing colonists— if, indeed, it *was* a clue. But what did it mean? Several interesting theories have arisen over the years. It is possible that one of these theories actually holds the key to the mystery.

The first and most unlikely theory holds that the settlers were

slaughtered by Indians. But while most of the Indians in the immediate area were hostile, no evidence of such a massacre ever was found.

The same is true of the theory that Roanoke Island was invaded by Spanish sailors who killed the colonists. It would have been virtually impossible for a massacre to have taken place without leaving some signs of a struggle. But there were no skeletons, no body parts, no weapons—not even bullet holes in the houses, trees, or walls of the fort to indicate that a violent encounter had occurred.

Governor White, although anxious to learn the fate of his family, was at least encouraged by the lack of signs of violence. He believed that, for unknown reasons, the settlers had moved away from Roanoke Island to live with friendly Indians—the Croatan tribe, who lived in an area south of Roanoke Island.

Governor White never found his loved ones or the other lost colonists. Eventually forced to return to England, he was unable to raise the necessary funds for another trip back to America. He died in 1593. But some evidence exists that the governor may have been correct.

It is known that, sometime around 1650, many Indians living in the vicinity of Roanoke Island moved inland and settled along the Lumber River in what today is Robeson County, North Carolina. Among these Indians was the Croatan tribe.

It is also known that when, in 1719, a group of white hunters visited the Robeson County area for the first time, they were greeted by a group of friendly, light-skinned Indians who spoke English. These Indians told the hunters that their ancestors had been able to, as they put it, "talk in books"—which meant that they could read. Some of these Indians had blond hair and blue eyes, traits which no native American Indians possessed.

The hunters also found that many of these light-skinned Indians had English names. And when, in 1790, a census was taken in Robeson County for the first time, it was learned that, of the ninety-five family names of the missing colonists of Roanoke Island, fifty-four of those names were found among the Indians living in the Lumber River area. This could hardly have been a coincidence, since not even the white settlers living in North Carolina in 1790 had as high a percentage of family names which were the same as those of the "Lost Colony" settlers. (Lumber River is slightly more than 200 miles southwest and inland from Roanoke Island.)

Taken together, these facts provide a very interesting theory of what actually may have happened to the lost colonists of Roanoke Island.

Sometime shortly after Governor White and his men sailed for England to bring back additional supplies for the settlement, *something* caused the colonists to abandon their settlement on Roanoke Island and move elsewhere. This unknown something may have been bad weather—Governor White and his crew left at the onset of what is known in the South as "hurricane season"—or (and this is a more likely explanation) it could have been frequent Indian attacks that forced the remaining settlers to leave their new homes behind.

At any rate, according to this theory the settlers left Roanoke Island with the Croatan Indians, whether willingly or as slaves. When the Croatan tribe finally settled in Robeson County, the colonists stayed with them there, too. And over the years, as colonists and Indians lived together, intermarried, and adopted one another's names, customs, and language, the result was a tribe that had mingled the qualities of both groups.

That's the theory, anyway. It is based largely on the one-word message left behind by the settlers: *Croatoan*. And because no one knows what actually happened to Virginia Dare or the lost colonists, that theory seems as good as any other. Probably it is as close to the truth as we'll ever get.

THE MYSTERY OF THE MARY CELESTE

THE *MARY CELESTE* WAS A LOVELY SHIP, A TALL AND STATELY SAILING vessel. A 206-ton, two-masted square rigger, she was captained by a capable, experienced New Englander named Benjamin Spooner Briggs.

On November 5, 1872, the *Mary Celeste* set sail from New York. Bound for Genoa, Italy, she was carrying a cargo of whiskey in her hold. Aboard the ship were ten people: Captain Briggs, his wife, their two-year-old daughter, and a crew of seven men.

Ten days after the *Mary Celeste* sailed out of New York harbor, another ship, the *Dei Gratia*, also left New York. She was bound for the British port of Gibraltar. Her captain, David Morehouse, was a close friend of Benjamin Briggs.

On December 5, 1872, the *Dei Gratia* was somewhere between Portugal and the Azores Islands when her crew sighted a ship in the distance ahead. It was the *Mary Celeste*. She was far off-course, and she appeared to be drifting aimlessly with the wind. As the *Dei Gratia* drew nearer, Captain Morehouse saw no signs of life aboard the other vessel, and no one at the helm. He ordered a lifeboat crew to board the *Mary Celeste.*

The boarding party searched the *Mary Celeste* thoroughly, but found no one at all on the ship. The lifeboats were missing, but there were no other clues as to what might have happened to the captain, his family, and the seven crew members.

The missing lifeboats indicated that the people aboard the *Mary Celeste* must have left in the face of some grave danger or difficulty—but what could it have been? There was a small amount of water in the hold, but the ship was still in good sailing condition; it had not sprung any serious leaks. The bilge pumps were in good working order, and the water was easily pumped out of the hold by the *Dei Gratia* crew. Enough food and drinking water remained to meet the needs of those who had been aboard the *Mary Celeste* for several months.

The windows had been boarded up and sealed with cloth and canvas. This led Captain Morehouse to wonder if perhaps the *Mary Celeste* had been tossed by stormy seas, or swamped by a huge wave which swept the crew and passengers overboard. But no—a small container of oil and an open bottle were found standing upright on tables in the captain's cabin. A child's nightgown lay nearby; it was dry, as was the rest of the clothing found on the ship. Razors belonging to the crewmen were not rusty, as they should have been if the ship had been swamped by a wave.

Other puzzles were equally perplexing.

The captain's table had been set for breakfast; one of the plates still had food on it. In the galley, pots containing food being prepared for meals still hung in place above the stove. In the first mate's cabin, an unfinished note was found lying on his desk. Hastily scribbled, it read, "My dear wife . . ."

These facts convinced Captain Morehouse that those aboard the *Mary Celeste* had been interrupted suddenly and without warning, and that they had been forced to abandon ship shortly thereafter. But what could have caused such a panic among the captain and crew? Whatever it was, it must have posed a severe threat to their lives; after all, the last thing in the world they would want to do in the open sea was to leave the safety of their ship and set out in the lifeboats.

Could the *Mary Celeste* have fallen victim to pirates? Possibly, except that there were no signs of violence on board the ship, and valuables such as gold, jewelry, money, and the whiskey cargo had not been taken. None of the cabins' contents were disturbed as they should have been if pirates had searched the ship. The only things missing from the ship were the ten persons who had set sail from New York and a few of the ship's instruments.

Another suggestion was that perhaps some of the alcohol stored in the hold had exploded. But the crew of the *Dei Gratia* found no evidence of an explosion or fire aboard the *Mary Celeste*.

By far the most popular theory was that the crew had broken into the ship's hold—an empty barrel of whiskey was found by the *Dei Gratia* crew—after which they had become drunk, murdered the captain and his wife and daughter, and left the ship in lifeboats. But no signs of a struggle were found, and none of the crew was ever seen again, either. If in fact a mutiny occurred aboard the *Mary Celeste*, the crewmen must have perished at sea in their lifeboats.

Finally, satisfied that he had done all he could to solve the mystery, Captain Morehouse assigned part of his own crew to the *Mary Celeste*, and on December 13 the two ships arrived in Gibraltar. The captain requested salvage rights for bringing in the abandoned ship, and an inquiry was held. At that inquiry, it was suggested that the crew of the *Dei Gratia* might have murdered everyone aboard the *Mary Celeste* in order to collect the salvage money. But the evidence denied any such finding—for instance, both vessels were sailing ships, and the *Dei Gratia* had left New York ten days after the *Mary Celeste*; how could it have managed to catch her in the open seas? Faced with a total lack of evidence of guilt, the court eventually awarded a small salvage fee to the *Dei Gratia*, and the case was closed.

For a while, that is.

In 1884, a little-known doctor wrote an account of the *Mary Celeste* mystery. The doctor was Arthur Conan Doyle, who later gained worldwide fame as the creator of Sherlock Holmes, the detective. After Doyle's story of the *Marie Celeste* (as he called it) was published, interest in the mystery was revived. Soon, the public was treated to an endless string of silly books devoted to bizarre theories about the disappearance of Captain Briggs, his family, and the crew of the *Mary Celeste*. Among those theories:

• The ship was attacked by a giant octopus, squid, or other sea monster.

• The ship went through a waterspout or whirlwind that sucked everyone out of their quarters and off the decks.

• A member of the crew was a crazed killer who murdered everyone on board the *Mary Celeste*. Then he flung himself into the sea and drowned.

• Everyone on board died of the bubonic plague or some other deadly disease. (Before dying, they must have leaped or been thrown into the sea, one by one, until none was left on board.)

• The ship sailed near an island that had only recently risen from the sea. Everyone left the ship to explore the island, whereupon the island sank and drowned them.

• The captain, crew, and passengers were captured and taken away by alien beings aboard a UFO. (This theory is silly be-

cause, unlike the next story in this book, there is absolutely no evidence whatever that any kind of UFO visitation might have occurred. In this case, the author of this particular theory might just as well have blamed UFOs for his having a wart on the end of his nose!)

• Some type of rare fungus developed within the ship's wooden timbers. Spores, or tiny seeds, of this fungus were released into the air, poisoning everyone aboard the *Mary Celeste*. Possibly maddened or made senseless by the poison, the crew and passengers flung themselves overboard and drowned in the sea.

Perhaps the wildest story of all was offered by a London teacher named Howard Linford. In a 1913 article, Linford told of a man named Abel Fosdyk who claimed to have been a stowaway and secret survivor of the *Mary Celeste* voyage.

According to Fosdyk's story, Captain Briggs had built a platform that extended out beyond the bow of the *Mary Celeste*. He built the platform for his young daughter to play on.

One day the captain and first mate began arguing about their ability to swim while fully clothed. As the argument grew heated, the captain suddenly leaped into the water and began to swim around the ship. Soon two other men joined him. Suddenly one of the men let out a shriek of pain: he was being attacked by sharks.

Everyone on board the *Mary Celeste* was drawn to the scene by the sailor's agonized screaming. As they crowded onto the newly-built platform, their combined weight caused the platform to collapse, sending them plunging into the mass of feeding sharks.

As for Mr. Fosdyk — he claimed that he alone had been able to climb onto a section of the platform as it floated in the sea. He clung to it while the sharks fed and the *Mary Celeste* drifted away. Finally, after days of drifting alone in the ocean, he washed up onto a beach on the northwestern coast of Africa.

And if you believe *that* story, you'll believe anything! There were more holes in Abel Fosdyk's tale than you'd find in a volleyball net. For example, Mr. Fosdyk neglected to mention why the lifeboats were missing. And if the boat drifted away from Mr. Fosdyk as he said, it would have been moving while the captain and two crewmen were trying to swim around it, too. Certainly the captain would have known that he could not swim fast enough while fully clothed to keep pace with the ship, much less to swim around her.

(On the other hand, if the captain really *was* stupid enough to build a platform that extended beyond the ship's deck for his two-year-old daughter to play on, he may have been stupid enough to try anything. But by all accounts, Captain Briggs was a level-headed, sensible man.)

No one knows what really happened to the ten people who were aboard the *Mary Celeste*. None of them was ever seen again after the ship left New York harbor on November 5, 1872. The captain's final log entry was dated November 24. In it, he listed the ship's location as being north of St. Mary's Island in the Azores. This position was 400 miles west of where she was found drifting ten days later by the *Dei Gratia*.

According to Captain Morehouse, it was impossible that the *Mary Celeste* could have drifted unmanned from her location on November 24 to where he found her on December 5. Her sails were set in such a manner that the wind would have taken her roughly 45 degrees north of the *Dei Gratia*, which was sailing in a southeasterly route into the wind. (Ships sail into the wind by a zigzag method known as tacking.) The *Mary Celeste* and the *Dei Gratia* were following the same route toward Gibraltar, but for the last 400 miles their sails had been set to tack in opposite directions. Thus, Captain Morehouse was astonished to find the *Mary Celeste* in his path rather than hundreds of miles away to the north, where she should have been according to the position of her sails.

This, then, was the mystery of the *Mary Celeste*: she was found, drifting and abandoned, in a part of the Atlantic Ocean where she should not have been unless someone had steered her there.

Her crew of ten sailors and passengers was gone, as were the lifeboats. All evidence pointed to a hasty departure from the ship—but for no apparent reason. There was no sign of violence or other unusual behavior on the part of anyone aboard the *Mary Celeste*.

Aside from the first mate's unfinished note and the captain's log entry of November 24, no message had been left behind to indicate where the lifeboats and their passengers might have gone. It was almost as if, in the middle of breakfast, everyone aboard the *Mary Celeste* had decided to disappear from the face of the earth.

Along with the famous story of the *Flying Dutchman*, the story of the *Mary Celeste* ranks among the most famous of all mysteries at sea.

That's hardly surprising, though. After all, it must have been a baffling mystery if Sherlock Holmes's creator could not solve it.

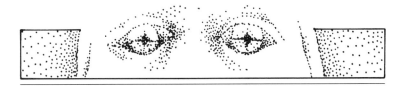

VISITORS FROM
ANOTHER WORLD

On September 19, 1961, Barney and Betty Hill were traveling by car along Route 3 in the White Mountains of New Hampshire. The Hills were tired and eager to get home: they were returning from a brief vacation in Canada, and they had been on the road for several hours.

It was nearly midnight and Barney was driving when he noticed a bright light in the clear sky outside the car. At first he thought it was a star. But then, as the car made its way around a series of sharp curves in the winding mountain road, Barney noticed that the star was still there, above and to one side of the car, regardless of which direction he turned. It seemed to be following their car. Barney pointed out the strange light to his wife, and they watched it for several miles.

Then, near the town of Whitefield, New Hampshire, the light

disappeared. Soon the Hills saw a strange craft on the ground a short distance ahead of them. Convinced that it must be a UFO (Unidentified Flying Object) that had landed, Barney stopped the car. He got out his binoculars and began to study the object.

In his later reports to the authorities, Barney described the craft as being about sixty-five feet wide, and shaped like a disk with two rows of windows and a red light on one side. Using the binoculars, he could see small, humanlike figures standing at the windows and watching him.

Barney had seen enough. He rushed back to the car and drove away at high speed.

Before the Hills had gone very far, though, they felt their car beginning to shake and vibrate wildly. They heard an odd, beeping sound, and suddenly they felt very sleepy . . .

And just as suddenly they were fully awake again as the beeping stopped. Barney was still driving, but the surroundings outside were different, unfamiliar to him and to Betty. Gradually, the Hills realized that they were thirty-five miles south of where they ought to be.

They discovered, too, that two hours had passed since the beeping had begun. Neither Barney nor Betty had any idea what had happened during those lost two hours.

The Hills reported their strange encounter to officials at Pease Air Force Base, and also to a Washington, D.C., research group which investigated UFO sightings. Then they tried to forget the whole thing. But they could not forget.

During the next two years, Betty Hill's sleep was often disturbed by frightening dreams. In her nightmares, she was aboard an alien spacecraft, being studied by strange, vaguely human creatures.

Barney Hill, too, suffered from the puzzling memory loss he had experienced during those two missing hours of his life. He developed nervous disorders (including a stomach ulcer) which finally, in December, 1963, drove him to seek the help of a psychiatrist, Dr. Benjamin Simon.

Dr. Simon was well known and highly respected in his field. When Barney Hill went to Boston to see him, the doctor suggested that both Barney and Betty undergo hypnotism in order to find out where the roots of their problem lay.

The process is known as *hypnotic regression*. It is based on the idea that our minds are like computers; that is, when something goes into our memory banks, it stays there forever. We may not be able to recall everything that has ever happened to us, but the facts are there, stored away in our brain, if we can only get at them.

Hypnosis is thought to be the key to reaching those distant, forgotten memories. Under hypnosis, the subject's mind can be unlocked to recall any of the millions of events in his past which have been pushed aside by other, more recent events. (For instance, can you recall what you got for Christmas when you were five years old? Perhaps you could, if you were hypnotized and taken back to that time in your life by a trained professional hypnotist. You could "see" the events unfolding in your mind exactly as they happened back then.)

Barney and Betty Hill accepted Dr. Simon's suggestion. In February, 1964, they allowed him to hypnotize them separately, so that the doctor could compare their versions of what happened to them on the night of September 19, 1961.

The story they revealed to Dr. Simon under hypnosis was, for lack of a better word, simply *incredible*.

First, it's important to realize that, under hypnosis, a person does not tell lies; rather, he tells the truth as he sees it. What he says may not actually be true, but *he believes it to be true*. So if he says something that sounds false, it is because he believes that what he is saying is true.

With that in mind, what did the Hills say under hypnosis about that September night in 1961?

When the beeping sound stopped (they said), they were on an unknown, lonely road. There was no other traffic on the road whatever. The engine of their car shut off as they found themselves drawing near a landed spacecraft of some kind. A group of strange, humanlike creatures appeared, took them from their car, and led them aboard the UFO.

According to the Hills, the creatures were less than five feet tall, with gray skin. They were wearing dark clothing (probably uniforms). Their heads were triangular, wide at the top and narrow at the chin. Their eyes were large and oval. They had no ears or noses, only slits where their nostrils should have been and holes where their ears should have been. Their mouths were not like ours, either, and they didn't seem to need them. They communicated with the Hills by making odd sounds that didn't sound like a language at all—yet the Hills said they could understand everything that was said to them. It was (they said) as if they were hearing in English inside their heads what the aliens were saying by making those odd noises.

While aboard the spacecraft, Barney and Betty Hill were separated and examined carefully by the alien visitors. The creatures appeared surprised that Barney's teeth came out—he wore false teeth—while Betty's did not.

When the examination was over, the Hills were reunited and told that they would remember nothing of what had happened aboard the spacecraft. Then the beeping began again . . . and the Hills found themselves on the road, two hours later and thirty-five miles away from where they were when they first saw the UFO.

Ever since the Hills told their story, people have wondered about it. Was it really true? There are many arguments against their account. And certainly the most common (and effective) arguments against any visits to Earth by beings from outer space also apply to the creatures in the Hills' story.

First, why would beings from outer space come this far from home, only to spend a couple of hours studying the Hills aboard their spacecraft before letting them go? That's like driving all the way from Alaska to Florida to visit Disney World and

EPCOT Center, and then staying only five minutes before packing up to go home again.

Second, since the aliens' intentions obviously were friendly — or at least they were not unfriendly — why didn't they attempt to share information with the Hills (and with the rest of the world as well)? Yet no one has ever produced any object other than moon rocks or meteorites which can be shown scientifically not to be of earthly origin.

Third, if these so-called aliens from other worlds are interested in studying planet Earth and its inhabitants, why do they never ask to be taken to world leaders such as the President of the United States, or to leading scientists who could help them to fulfill their mission?

Other arguments concern the Hills' story itself. First, people driving at night on long trips often become drowsy and lose their sense of time. Barney Hill and his wife could have gotten sleepy, made a wrong turn somewhere along the way, and failed to realize where they were until two hours later when they became alert again.

Also, many psychiatrists do not consider hypnotism to be a trustworthy method of obtaining evidence. For instance, the Hills could have discussed what it would be like to be kidnapped by beings from outer space before they were hypnotized. They could have made up the entire story, and then convinced themselves that it was true. If so, their stories under hypnosis would appear to be true. People do not tell lies under hypnosis — but they will tell what they honestly believe to be the truth.

On the other hand, there are reasons to believe the Hills' strange story. First of all, Benjamin Simon, the doctor who hypnotized the Hills, is a highly respected, trained, and experienced professional. Dr. Simon would have known if the Hills were "faking" their hypnotic trances. And through careful questioning, he determined to his own satisfaction that they had not made up their fantastic story. As far as he was (and is) concerned, their story was genuine.

The Hills were hypnotized separately, not together. Their stories agreed in every major respect. While their stories did not agree in every minor detail, Dr. Simon considered the differences to be normal. (In fact, he would have been suspicious if their separate stories had agreed in every instance, because no two observers ever see exactly the same thing.)

Under hypnosis, Betty Hill recalled a particular physical examination technique which she said the aliens had used on her—yet no such medical technique existed on earth at the time. It was not until ten years later that doctors began using a similar technique with their patients for the first time.

While she was hypnotized, Betty Hill also drew a "star map" which she said she had been shown while she and her husband were aboard the spacecraft. The visitors from outer space explained to her that lines on the map which connected certain stars indicated trade routes and visits to other worlds. Betty, who knew no more about astronomy than the average person, had no idea where the star system shown on the map was located; in fact, she did not even know whether such a star system really existed.

Five years later, in 1969, an amateur astronomer found just such a pattern in a star system known as Zeta Reticuli. And while not every astronomer agrees with this finding, it suggests that Betty's story might be true.

Finally, there is the fact that Betty and Barney Hill had little to gain and much to lose from the publicity surrounding their weird story of encountering other-worldly beings. The Hills were a married interracial couple—Betty was white, Barney black—at a time when widespread public acceptance of interracial marriage was still in the future. (In 1961, when the Hills experienced their strange encounter, some states still had laws against interracial marriages.) It is hard to believe that a well-to-do, middle-aged couple would invite added attention—and, possibly, public displeasure and ridicule as well—by making up a bizarre story of a UFO kidnapping. It is equally hard to believe that both of them could have fooled as capable and respected a physician as Dr. Simon.

Did Barney and Betty Hill actually encounter a group of alien beings twenty-five years ago? Were they taken aboard the alien spacecraft and later released unharmed, but with no conscious memory of the event? They are the only ones who know for sure, whether consciously or subconsciously.

As for us—well, it boils down to whether each of us believes in the existence of UFOs and extraterrestrial beings. We should all remember two things, though: just because we *don't* believe in UFOs does not mean that they don't exist. And just because we *do* believe in them does not mean that we are weird or crazy.

THE VANISHING MAN

OF ALL THE STRANGE AND OFTEN FRIGHTENING STORIES IN THIS book, none is stranger or more frightening than this one. It is strange because no one has even the remotest idea of exactly what happened to David Lang on the hot, dry afternoon of September 23, 1880; it's frightening because, for all we know, the same thing could happen to anyone—even you or me!

David Lang wiped his brow, glanced at the skies, and frowned as he and his wife stepped out of their brick farmhouse. It was another scorching hot day. The sun beamed down unmercifully from a cloudless sky overhead. The Langs' two children—Sarah, aged eleven, and George, eight—were playing in the front yard with a toy their father had brought them from Nashville that morning.

David was worried. Like many other farmers in middle Tennessee, he was wondering when a break in the hot weather would bring much-needed rain to water his fields and crops.

The entire area around Gallatin, Tennessee, was suffering the effects of a long dry spell.

"I think I'll take a look at the fields," David told his wife. She nodded and walked over to talk with the children.

David frowned again as he entered his forty-acre pasture. Normally, the pasture was filled with green grasses; now, though, it was brown and lifeless from a lack of rain.

David Lang walked aimlessly for a while, and then he paused. Several hundred yards behind him, his wife and children were clearly in view in the front yard. Nearer to him, and also in full view, a horse-drawn buggy was turning into the lane that bordered the pasture and led to the Langs' farmhouse. Inside the buggy were Judge August Peck and another man, Peck's brother-in-law. David waved to them. He turned toward the farmhouse. His wife and children were watching the approaching buggy.

Judge Peck, who was driving the buggy, saw David standing alone in the open pasture. He began to lift his arm to wave to him, and was preparing to call out, when suddenly David vanished.

The judge's first thought was that David must have fallen into a hole or crack in the dry ground, since there were no trees in the grassy pasture to hide him from view. And because of the dry weather, the grass was too short to conceal his body if he had fainted or suffered a heart attack.

Mrs. Lang, too, had seen her husband disappear. She gave a small cry of alarm and ran toward the spot where he had been standing. George and Sarah followed her, wondering what had happened to their father. Soon, all five people were gathered at the scene—but there was no hole in the ground, and no sign of David Lang. He was gone, and no one knew where he had gone. Or how. Or why.

Mrs. Lang began to scream and cry uncontrollably. The two

men led her and the children back to the house; then they rang
the alarm bell in the yard which was used to alert neighbors in
cases of emergencies such as fires.

Within minutes, neighbors began to arrive. They were joined
by later arrivals as word spread quickly throughout the area that
help was urgently needed at the Lang farm. Soon, scores of
searchers were carefully going over every square inch of the
pasture and surrounding land.

They found no trace of David Lang, nothing at all that could
explain his mysterious disappearance. There were no holes in
the ground, no cracks in the earth that he might have fallen into.
He had disappeared in plain sight of five people, and no one
could offer even the slightest clue as to his whereabouts.

The search continued for several weeks without success. A
professional geologist was called in to examine the field. He
described it as "topsoil covering a limestone bedrock." And
while limestone is a porous rock filled with tiny holes like
a hardened sponge, the geologist found no trace of holes or
cracks in the bedrock beneath the meadow where David Lang
disappeared.

The mystery quickly grew famous as newspapers reported
details of the bizarre case. Curious sightseers came from far and
wide to view the place where a man had vanished from the face
of the earth. For a while, armed guards were necessary to keep
people away from the farm. Before long, though, the crowds
began to dwindle as what had been an exciting novelty gradually became old news. Eventually, the crowds went away
altogether and life returned to normal in the Lang household—
at least, it was as normal as could be expected under the
circumstances.

Some things, though, never were quite the same. And some
things were even more mysterious than before.

When the following spring arrived in middle Tennessee, rain

was plentiful and the grass in David Lang's pasture was green and healthy. Cattle grazed contentedly in the lush field—but none would touch the grass near the spot where David had vanished. Within a circular area twenty feet in diameter where he had stood in his last moments on earth, the grass grew thick and tall, ignored by the feeding animals. It was said that not even insects bothered that tiny plot of pastureland.

One day in August, 1881, the two Lang children were walking in the meadow. Their mother was in the house, and no one else was around. Twelve-year-old Sarah, who like the others had never gotten over the loss of her father, called out, "Father, where are you?" There was no answer.

She repeated her question, louder this time. She and George listened intently for some kind of reply, but still there was no answer. She called out to her father twice more, with the same results.

Sarah looked at her younger brother and shrugged her shoulders. He shook his head sadly. It was useless. After all, Father had been gone for nearly a year.

But then, as the children turned to walk away, they heard a man's voice.

"*Help!*" the voice called faintly, as if it were coming from somewhere far away.

The two children stared at each other in amazement. Could it be . . . ?

"It's Father!" Sarah cried. She and George turned and raced back to the farmhouse, shouting for their mother as they went. They explained breathlessly what they had heard. Mrs. Lang and the children ran back to the meadow.

Standing in the center of the tall grass where her husband had disappeared, Mrs. Lang called out loudly, "David, is it you?"

"*Yes*," the voice replied. All three of the Langs burst into tears of happiness and relief. For nearly a year they had been hoping that he would return to them from wherever he had gone.

"Where are you?" Mrs. Lang managed to ask between sobs. He sounded so close to them.

"*I don't know*," he replied. His voice, already faint, was fading like the signal of a distant radio station.

"Come back to us!" Mrs. Lang shouted. But it was no use. Her husband was gone again.

For several days thereafter, Mrs. Lang and the children returned to the meadow. On each occasion, they were able to communicate briefly with David Lang. But with every passing day his voice grew even more distant and indistinct than before. Finally, it disappeared entirely, just as he had done almost a year earlier.

That was the last anyone ever heard from David Lang.

What happened to David Lang? Not even he, speaking through his disembodied voice, could answer that question.

No one else can answer it, either.

Mrs. Lang seemed to think that her husband's body simply burst or broke apart, "like a soap bubble," as she put it. (Why his body might explode in such a manner, or do so without making a sound, she had no idea; still, in a case like this, in which practically nothing makes sense anyway, one more unexplained occurrence is hardly unreasonable.) But one nagging question remains: If David Lang's body somehow burst into billions of tiny particles, how could he have managed to talk with her and the children a year later?

A second theory devised to account for David Lang's sudden disappearance is that he was beamed aboard an alien spacecraft. But in order for this to be true, several factors would have to be taken into account.

First, the UFO would have had to be invisible, since no one saw any such alien spacecraft in the clear sky overhead. Or else the UFO, stationed somewhere beyond the vision of the five witnesses, must have used an "invisible ray" to render Mr. Lang invisible and beam him aboard the spacecraft.

Second, the spacecraft would have had to remain within communication range of the Lang farm for eleven months.

Third, David Lang would have required access, however brief, to the aliens' radio or communication system in order to speak with his family.

Fourth, either David Lang or his alien captors would have had to be listening at the precise moment when Sarah called out to her father.

While all of those conditions *may* have existed, we have no reason to believe that any of them actually did exist. There was no evidence of any sort of mysterious, UFO-type activity in the Gallatin, Tennessee, area around 1880. So while UFOs may or may not actually exist—Barney and Betty Hill certainly believed that they did—we cannot say they are real simply because David Lang vanished one day under mysterious circumstances.

Finally, there is the theory that somehow, in a manner unknown to us, David Lang moved into another dimension of time and space of which we are unaware. He may have accidentally slipped into another level of existence which presently is unknown to us.

Death is one such unknown. We live, we die—and what then? Is there some kind of life or existence beyond ours? The major religions of the world teach us that death is not the final step; so does spiritualism.

Ghosts are another such unknown: they are thought by many people to be the restless spirits of those who no longer reside among the living.

Regardless of whether we believe in ghosts or an afterlife, the possibility of their existence is real. We may not understand them fully, but that does not mean that they are not real. No one understands why aspirins cure headaches, either—but they do.

Of the three theories concerning David Lang's disappearance, the last seems the most logical. Still, we'll probably never know if David Lang actually entered a different plane of existence from our own, or what that existence might be like.

One thing is sure, though: if he ever comes back from wherever he went, he'll have an interesting story to tell.

Unexplained
Mysteries
Around Us

THE MYSTERY OF
THE NAZCA LINES

LET'S SUPPOSE THAT OUR ASSIGNMENT IN ART CLASS TODAY WAS TO make a simple drawing of a spider. Could we do it?

First, we might start by drawing a circle or oval shape. (That would be the spider's body.) Then we'd draw another, smaller circle—the spider's head—attached to its body. Finally, we'd add eight legs, four on either side.

But what if the teacher made the assignment harder? What if we had to make the drawing in one continuous line, without lifting our pencils from the paper once we'd begun? Or what if she took us outside onto the school's playground, gave us shovels to dig with, and told us to "draw" the spider's outline by digging in one long, continuous line? (And to make it even tougher, when we were finished the spider had to be fifty yards long from one end to the other.) Could we still do it? And would our "drawing" look like a spider when we were finished? Maybe, and maybe not.

Two things are certain, though: it would be extremely hard work, and our "drawing" would remain for a long time after we put away our shovels and went home to take a bath.

Such a "drawing" depicting a spider one hundred and fifty feet long actually exists, in South America. It's found in southern Peru, in a hot, dry region known as the Plain of Nazca. Along with more than a hundred other, similar "drawings" of snakes, monkeys, hummingbirds, jaguars, condors, llamas, whales, fish, seabirds, and flowers that have been made in the rocky desert, the huge spider is but one small part of a much larger mystery: the fascinating, unsolved enigma of the Nazca Lines.

The mystery begins in an area known as the Bay of Pisco, where the Pacific Ocean meets the coast of Peru. There, where rusty-red mountains crowd the narrow shoreline, one mountain is of particular interest. Midway up its steep, smooth, treeless slopes, an enormous figure has been carved out of the rocky mountain face. This figure consists of three long, perfectly straight paths which are joined near the base and contain other shorter, curved paths. Together, they stretch upward for three hundred feet or more in the thousand-foot face of the mountain. Scientists say that the figure definitely is man-made, and that it is between five hundred and two thousand years old.

If we were to stand at the top or bottom of the mountain, we could not see the figure at all. And if we were to stand on the mountainside, we could see only a small portion of the huge figure at one time. We could not possibly guess what the lines are for. But if we were to fly over the mountains in an airplane at an altitude of, say, one thousand feet, we would be able to identify the carving immediately: it is a *trident*—a three-pronged spear or pitchfork. Its prongs seem to be pointing inland southeast of the Bay of Pisco.

Why, we might ask ourselves, should the carved trident point toward Nazca? After all, few people live there now. The heat is intense, and the area receives only one quarter inch of annual rainfall. Nazca is not exactly an ideal vacation spot, unless you're fascinated by ancient mysteries.

Because no one has offered a better explanation for the trident's existence, let's assume that its purpose was to point us toward the Nazca area. What would we find if we headed southeast from the Bay of Pisco, traveling inland to the hot, barren Plain of Nazca?

The Nazca Plain is a flat and lonely place. For a hundred miles in all directions, the ground is covered with countless millions of small, dark-colored rocks and pebbles. A few inches beneath the rocky, grassless surface, the ground is lighter colored, ranging from white to tan to yellowish. As we have noted, it seldom rains here, and the surface rocks protect the soil from wind and erosion.

A few small rivers and creeks flow through the area. Their riverbeds are dry throughout much of the year; only during the rainy seasons do they fill with water flowing from the Andes Mountains to the sea. Along these rivers and creeks small towns such as Nazca, Palpa, and El Ingenio struggle to survive. A paved road, the Pan-American Highway, stretches from Lima, Peru, southward to Chile. It passes through the Nazca area and even crosses some of the Nazca lines and figures.

Scattered over three hundred square miles of the Nazca Plain are more than one hundred enormous figures—mostly animals, birds and plants—which were created by persons unknown at some time in the distant past.

How the animals were formed is easily explained: the builders simply removed the darker rocks and pebbles at the surface and laid them aside, revealing the lighter ground inches below. But all of the figures are large. Some are six hundred feet long, and as wide as a football field. Most of the markings consist of a single, narrow line that does not cross itself, the way our art teacher wanted us to draw the spider. They must have been incredibly difficult to create.

These "drawings" in the desert are, for the most part, remarkably accurate: for example, a monkey with a long, curving tail, and a hummingbird with a long bill, wings, and tail-feathers. But each of the monkey's hands measures forty feet across, and its body is two hundred fifty feet long.

If we were standing amid the lines that make up the monkey's tail, all we would see is a shallow, spiraling line six to twelve inches wide where stones have been moved aside. We certainly could not identify the lines as being part of a monkey's tail. The only way we could possibly recognize the monkey or any of the other animal figures on the Plain of Nazca would be to view them from the air.

Thus, additional mysteries arise: *With neither mountains nor aircraft to view the figures from above or direct the artists' work, how could the ancient artists have made such accurate drawings on such a large scale? And who was meant to see artwork that, when viewed from the ground, looks like nothing more than shallow lines and paths that have been dug out of the earth?*

Pottery remains found in the area date back to people who lived in the Nazca region between 100 B.C. and 700 A.D. Perhaps the "drawings" were made by these primitive people to be seen by their gods in the sky. This is only a guess, however; no one knows for sure why the animal "drawings" were created, or how they were "drawn" so accurately in view of their huge size and the limited skills of the ancient people who created them.

The Nazca region is a land of mystery—but its most puzzling mysteries do not involve figures carved on mountainsides, or even animal figures dug into the rocky desert ground. Rather, they involve a vast network of millions of straight lines of all sizes which have been painstakingly dug out of the desert over

hundreds of square miles of the flat Nazca Plain. These lines, which form triangles, rectangles, and other figures, are set at all sorts of odd angles to each other. These are the famous Nazca Lines. They represent one of the earth's oldest and most baffling, unexplained mysteries.

Some of the Nazca Lines are as narrow as four inches; others measure hundreds of yards across—large enough to have been seen by astronauts aboard Skylab II! In some cases the lines extend for miles without the slightest bend, even when passing over hills, valleys, and dry riverbeds. More than fifty of the lines are at least a mile long.

From the ground, the narrower lines look like nothing more than walking paths in the rocky terrain. In many cases, the lines cannot be seen at all from more than a few feet away. The wider lines appear to be merely large clearings where the rocks have been moved aside and piled in rows along the borders.

The paths and clearings are shallow; seldom are they deeper than three to four inches into the ground. Scientists who have studied the lines say that they could not possibly have been formed by wind, flowing water, or any other natural force.

How many lines are there? They number in the millions. They occur in all sizes and shapes, and they appear to have been laid out in random directions. In many cases, a single line has several other lines crossing it at angles—and *those* lines have other lines crossing them as well!

The Nazca Lines are found mainly in an area that is thirty miles long and ten miles wide. This area is located between the towns of Nazca and Palpa in southern Peru, and two hundred miles south of Lima, the capital of Peru.

People have known about the strange markings in the Nazca Plain for hundreds of years. Until recent times, though, few people were curious as to their purpose. The lines in the desert were not considered important because no one knew what they were. It was not until the late 1920s, when the figures were first viewed from the air, that people became excited about what they meant.

From the air, the meaningless, curved lines magically turned into flower petals and whales' tails and seabirds' wings.

From the air, the razor-straight paths and clearings in the desert looked exactly like the crisscrossing runways of a modern airport!

And that's why the Nazca Lines are so famous: their mystery has captured the imagination of the entire world.

After all, why would people take the time and effort necessary to create a huge network of runway-like, rectangular clearings that crisscross three hundred square miles of desert like unfinished tic-tac-toe games? After all, it wasn't until 1903 that the Wright Brothers actually flew their airplane for the first time. Until then, there was no way to view the Nazca Lines from overhead.

As we have seen, scientists know *how* the Nazca Lines were created. (By moving millions of tons of small rocks aside to create paths or clearings which reveal the lighter colored ground beneath the stones.) And scientists think they know, too, how old most of the lines are, and who "drew" them. (They were created by people who lived in the Nazca area between 1,300 to 2,100 years ago.)

What scientists don't know is, Why were the lines drawn in the first place?

At least three possible answers have been given.

At least two of the answers probably are dead wrong.

The first theory concerning the Nazca Lines is that the stones were moved away in order to clear the land for farming. People who support this theory point out that what look like the remains of ancient irrigation canals have been found in a few places in the desert. But there are millions of man-made clearings of all sizes in the Nazca Plain, and only a handful of these "canals." Too, the animal figures were not created to provide farmland for the people who lived there: the figures are too large, and the lines too small, for farming to have been the reason for their creation.

A second and more widely held theory is that the Nazca Lines were some kind of "calendar of the sky." According to this theory, the lines pointed to the position of the sun, moon, stars, and planets at certain times of the year. Such a calendar, many experts say, would have been valuable to farmers, telling them when to plant and harvest their crops.

On the other hand, there are millions of lines pointing in every direction of the compass. A 1968 scientific study showed that some of the lines do seem to indicate the location of the sun, moon, stars, and planets on the horizon at certain times of the year. But the study also found that most of the lines do not point toward any particular heavenly object. The scientists concluded that the calendar theory was incorrect.

The third theory behind the Nazca Lines is the wildest theory of all. It's fantastic, almost unbelievable, but it *does* fit the facts and offer realistic answers to many questions—if you accept the theory.

According to this theory, the planet Earth once was visited by ancient astronauts from outer space. Why they might have chosen to land on the Plain of Nazca is unknown. But while they were here, they built huge runways and landing strips for their spacecraft—and they created the trident on the mountainside at the Bay of Pisco as a guide for other astronauts looking for the Plain of Nazca.

This theory also may explain how the people were able to "draw" their animal figures so large, yet so accurately: the visitors from outer space were able to guide them in their work. They could have used their aircraft to hover over the desert and direct the "drawings" from above.

Which of these three theories do you believe? The first two theories—that the Nazca Lines related to farming or the calendar—are easier to accept than the idea that beings from outer space once visited Earth.

But don't make up your mind before you read on!

Since scientists first began studying the Nazca area, they have found more than 200,000 clay pots used by the ancient people who lived there. Many of those pots were decorated with paintings of people whose skin color was white, yellow, red, brown, or black. And at one end of the high plain, primitive statues and carvings of human heads were found which showed those same racial features.

But how did the ancient Nazcans know that people existed on earth whose skin color was different from their own? After all, they had never seen white-skinned Europeans, or black-skinned Africans, or yellow-skinned Orientals. (The first white man to visit South America—Francisco Pizarro, a Spanish explorer—didn't arrive until 1531 A.D.)

If you accept the ancient astronaut theory, you might also believe that, when these space travelers came to Nazca, they brought with them knowledge of other races they had visited in other places on Earth.

When Pizarro reached Peru, he was surprised to find that the Indians of the mighty Inca Empire who ruled Peru at the time were expecting him. According to their legends, they had once been visited in the distant past by another white man named Viracocha, who came down from the skies in a fiery vehicle. Before he left, Viracocha told them that someday he would return.

Could that "fiery vehicle" have been a giant rocket?

One more interesting point remains concerning the Viracocha legend: the Incas said that he had a long, flowing, white beard. And that was strange because, like the American Indians, the Incas did not grow beards. If the Viracocha story was a legend and nothing more, how did the Incas know that beards existed? How did they know that white men sometimes wore them?

Among the many "drawings" in the Plain of Nazca are some which cannot be fully explained. For instance, the spider mentioned earlier is found, not in the Nazca region, but hundreds of miles away, beyond the mountains to the northeast. That particular kind of spider, which has an oddly formed third leg, is found nowhere on earth except in the thick, steamy Amazon jungles.

How did the Nazcans know that such a spider existed?

Other figures in the Nazca plain represent animals such as hump-backed camels and African lions with thick manes—but there are no such animals in all of South America, and never have been (except in modern-day zoos)! And one "drawing" of a llama (a relative of the camel) has, not two toes on each foot as llamas have today, but *five* toes. Scientists say that, once upon a time, llamas did have five toes on each foot—but that was at least ten thousand years ago! The oldest known remains of man's existence in the Nazca area date back no further than three thousand years.

Unanswered Questions • The ancient people of Nazca could not read or write. They had no alphabet, and no written language. They had no system of math as we have today. They used fire for warmth and to cook by, and they lived in houses rather than caves. They had not invented the wheel, and they built no roads to travel on from place to place. They were little more than simple farmers. Yet they built irrigation ditches to water their crops, and they created beautiful objects of ceramic pottery and painted them in bright colors with clever and appealing designs.

And for some reason which remains unexplained, they created millions of enormous designs and figures in the dry, windless Plain of Nazca. These designs, the famous "Nazca Lines" of Peru, are as mysterious as they are well known. Spread out over more than three hundred square miles of hot, rocky desert, these lines and figures are meaningless except when viewed from the air high above them. Then, as if by magic, they turn into all sorts of animals and other figures which look remarkably lifelike—or else they take on the appearance of a vast network of airport runways that is millions of times larger than New York's Kennedy International Airport.

Why did these primitive people invest the time and effort to create gigantic lines and figures which can be seen only from the sky? Was the Nazca area actually visited by some race of beings from outer space more than a thousand years ago? No one knows for sure. Maybe we'll never know.

All we can say at this point is that the earth is filled with unexplained mysteries. And none of them is more puzzling than the lingering mystery of the Nazca Lines of Peru.

THE IMPOSSIBLE EXPLOSION

WHEN MASSIVE EXPLOSIONS OCCUR ON EARTH, THEIR CAUSES ARE almost always known. Often eyewitnesses have described them in detail—or else, when no witnesses were present, scientists have carefully examined the evidence left at the scene in order to determine how the explosions occurred.

In 1908, however, an incredibly powerful explosion rocked a remote, forested region of Siberia—and to this day, scientists cannot agree as to what caused the explosion. Since the mysterious explosion occurred near the Stony Tunguska River, it has become known simply as the Tunguska Explosion.

It was shortly after sunrise—7:17 A.M., to be exact—on June 30, 1908, when the fireball was seen streaking across the cloudless sky over central Siberia. Witnesses to the event later stated that the fireball, which was brighter than the rising sun, crossed the sky in a matter of seconds and disappeared. Moments later, a blinding flash of white light appeared above the trees near the Stony Tunguska River. Residents of Kirensk, a city two hundred fifty miles away, described the flash as "a pillar of fire." It was accompanied by a thunderous, ear-shattering explosion that was heard as much as five hundred miles away.

The earth trembled with the force of the blast; buildings shook, windowpanes shattered, and men and animals were tossed around like toy figures. Forty miles from the scene of the explosion, a man's shirt was burned off his back and the blast knocked him off his front porch. At least two villages near the blast site were completely destroyed, and an entire herd of 1,500 reindeer was killed.

Siberia is, for the most part, a cold, remote, and lonely place. It occupies five million square miles of northwestern Russia.

The harsh land of northern Siberia is bitterly cold; like northern Alaska, it lies inside the Arctic circle and as a result much of its land is permanently frozen. In central Siberia, where the Tunguska Explosion occurred, the land also is cold and forbidding: residents herd reindeer in the same way that our western ranchers raise cattle. But central Siberia also contains the largest forests in the world—and it is these seemingly endless evergreen forests that provide an accurate picture of the awesome force generated by the explosion.

It was not until 1927, nineteen years after the explosion occurred, that scientists finally were able to reach the area and study the results of the mysterious blast. Their delay was due to two factors: an almost total absence of roads in central Siberia, and political unrest in Russia which led to the 1917 Revolution. What those scientists encountered when they arrived in the Tunguska region was almost beyond belief.

They found an area of four hundred square miles in which the forest had been virtually destroyed. As a local tribesman put it, "The fire came by and destroyed the forest, the reindeer, and all other animals."

Twenty miles from the blast site, they found countless millions of dead pine and fir trees which had been uprooted and leveled. As far as the eye could see, trees were stacked in rows with their trunks pointing like huge skeleton fingers toward the blast site.

Twelve miles from the site, the trees, still piled in neat rows pointing ahead, were burned and blackened.

Five miles away from the blast site, the charred, lifeless trees had been stripped of their bark and limbs. The complete absence of tree limbs convinced the scientists that the damage and burning had occurred instantly. (Fire would have destroyed the forest and burned the trees, including their limbs and bark, but it would not have blown down the trees, and it would not have stripped the bark and limbs from the trees.)

Finally, the scientists reached the precise point where the blast occurred: a circular area of blackened earth that measured twenty-five feet across. Outside this small area, the lifeless remains of evergreen trees lay pointing toward the center as before. But inside the tiny circle the silent, skeleton trees were still standing defiantly, as if whatever unknown force had blown down the other trees could not defeat them. It had peeled away their bark, ripped away their limbs, and created a small island of dead, *standing* tree trunks.

But why should this be so? Why should these trees and virtually no others stand like dead guardians over the countless millions of trees that had fallen in precise rows for twenty miles on every side of them?

The answer is simple, once you think about it: those trees were not blown down because the explosion occurred in the air directly overhead. While other trees for miles around were ripped out of the ground by their roots and folded back to lie in rows, the trees directly beneath the blast site were pushed *downward*, and not to one side, by the explosion.

But now, consider the most difficult question of all.

What Caused the Tunguska Explosion? · Scientists have estimated the force of the Tunguska Explosion to have been equal
to 12.5 megatons of TNT—nearly half as powerful as the volcanic eruption which destroyed the island of Krakatoa in 1883.
However, it could not have been a volcanic eruption that rocked
central Siberia in 1908: there were no volcanoes there, whether
active or inactive. Besides, witnesses reported seeing a fireball
hurtling across the sky just before the blast occurred.

Could the fireball have been a giant meteorite like the ones
that left enormous craters in Africa and Arizona? If so, it certainly did not act like a meteorite.

When large meteorites fall to earth, they explode with tre-
mendous force. Upon impact, they gouge huge craters out of
the earth and shatter into tiny fragments of rock that are sent
flying for considerable distances from the site. Yet no impact
crater was found anywhere in central Siberia and no fragments
of meteorites were ever found. And if, as the evidence suggests,
the explosion occurred in midair, there still should have been
meteorite remains scattered around the site for miles. But there
were none. No evidence was ever found to indicate that the blast
was due to a falling meteorite.

But if volcanoes and meteorites were not to blame, what else
might have caused the Tunguska Explosion?

Some scientists believe that it resulted from a collision between the earth and the tail of a comet. Other scientists who
disagree with this theory point out that a comet large enough to
survive a trip through Earth's upper atmosphere and still wipe
out four hundred square miles of forest should have been seen
by astronomers long before it approached our planet.

Some scientists have concluded that the Tunguska Explosion
was, in fact, a nuclear detonation of some sort. After all, it
certainly was powerful enough to have been a nuclear explosion; and some eyewitnesses reported seeing a column of fire,

smoke, or some kind of "mushroom-shaped cloud" rising high into the air after the blast occurred. The cloud was estimated by scientists to have risen thirty-two miles into the atmosphere.

The main problem with this theory is that, while the Siberian explosion occurred in 1908, scientists did not develop atomic weapons or devices until 1944–1945.

Russian scientist Aleksander Kazantsev has suggested that the Siberian explosion could have resulted from the destruction in midair of an alien spaceship whose atomic-powered engines developed serious problems as the craft was entering the earth's atmosphere and attempting to land. This theory would explain the fireball seen by witnesses, and other eyewitness reports as well which described the fireball as a round, solid object that changed direction in the sky, as if it were being steered before the blast occurred.

Other explanations that have been suggested as causes of the Tunguska Explosion—a collision between matter and antimatter from space, or a "black hole" that struck the earth—are too complex for us to consider here. The most we can say about them is that, for a variety of reasons, most scientists have rejected both of those theories as applied to the Tunguska incident. They are no more likely to be true in the case of the Tunguska Explosion than the "alien spacecraft" theory.

Thus, we are left with an impossible, incredibly powerful explosion which could not have occurred—yet it *did* occur, less than a century ago. It probably will remain one of the greatest unsolved natural mysteries in the earth's long history.

THE AMAZING MAP
OF PIRI REIS

IN 1929, WHILE THE FAMOUS TOPKAPI PALACE IN ISTANBUL, TURKEY, was undergoing repairs, workmen made a startling discovery. They found a map which, although it had been drawn four hundred years earlier, appeared to contain information that was unknown when the map was prepared. In fact, some of the map's remarkable features were not proven accurate until 1949, twenty years *after* the map was found in Topkapi Palace.

When Christopher Columbus set sail from Spain with his tiny fleet of three small ships and ninety men in 1492, he was searching for a western sea route to India.

Columbus never reached India—but when, on October 12, 1492, he landed on the small island of San Salvador, he discovered something far more valuable than a trade route to India: the vast and wealthy lands of the New World of North and South America.

Columbus's discovery soon led to widespread interest in the New World that lay across the Atlantic Ocean from Europe. Soon, other nations such as Portugal, England, and France began sending explorers to claim the uncharted land for their nations. It quickly became a race to see who could colonize the lands and claim their vast fortunes in gold and natural resources. Thus began the Age of Discovery, which lasted until well into the 1600s.

In 1513—twenty-one years after Columbus's first voyage to the New World—a Turkish naval officer named Piri Reis, or Admiral Piri, decided to have his map-makers prepare a map of the Atlantic Ocean and the lands bordering it.

At that time, map-making was hardly the exact science that it is today. Few if any accurate maps existed of the area, since only a handful of Europeans had ever crossed the Atlantic to see what lay on the other side. Piri Reis intended his map of the Atlantic Ocean and its lands to be the most precise and accurate ever drawn.

When the map was completed, Piri Reis added several handwritten messages of his own at various places on the map. In one place he mentioned that, in preparing his map, he and his map-makers studied many older existing maps which dated back as far as 300 B.C. Elsewhere he said that part of his map was based on those Columbus had used on his first voyage to the New World in 1492.

But how could that be true? If Columbus was the discoverer of the New World, how could he have used maps to find it unless someone else had visited the area before him? Remember, when Columbus set sail for India in 1492, most people believed that the earth was flat, not round as we know it to be. Many Europeans expected Columbus to sail off the earth's edge before he got very far.

Prior to 1492, maps of the western Atlantic Ocean were based on whatever the map-makers thought might be out there in the vast blue unknown. After Columbus's historic voyage, improvements in sea maps still came slowly. It was as if the world were a giant jigsaw puzzle with most of the pieces missing. Each explorer in his turn added what small bits he found to the overall understanding of what the world beyond the horizon was really like.

To the best of anyone's knowledge, neither Piri Reis nor the Turkish navy ever visited the lands far to the west that were shown on his map. His sailing voyages were confined to the Mediterranean Sea. Still, his map was remarkably accurate—more so than any other map of the Atlantic Ocean that existed at the time.

When the Piri Reis map was discovered in 1929, it quickly became a hot news item. Although it had been prepared more than four centuries earlier, it showed the continents of South America and Africa in their correct relative longitude—that is, it showed their coastlines and the distances between them with a high degree of precision and accuracy. There was simply no way that Piri Reis could have known these facts, since relatively little of the South American coastline had been charted by explorers in the twenty-one years since Columbus had landed in America.

A greater mystery concerning the Piri Reis map arose during the 1950s. Captain A. H. Mallery, a retired U. S. Navy officer, discovered that the bottom of the map showed the coastline of an area of Antarctica known as Queen Maud Land. There were two reasons why this should be considered unusual. First, in 1513 no one had ever seen Antarctica; in fact, at that time no one even knew that it existed. Antarctica was not discovered until three hundred years later, in 1818.

Second—and even more surprising—the coastline exists as shown on the map, but it lies buried beneath ice that is half a mile deep. It was not until 1949 that a multinational team of scientists was able to map the coastline under the ice of Queen Maud Land. Their maps, made by using the best and most modern scientific equipment available, are practically identical to the coastline of Antarctica that appears on the Piri Reis map

drawn in 1513. Yet this polar ice cap has covered the coast of Queen Maud Land for 15,000 years or more.

How could Piri Reis have known about Antarctica in 1513 when it was not discovered until 1818? And how could he have accurately mapped the Antarctic coastline when it has been hidden from view beneath half a mile of ice for more than 15,000 years?

Another aspect of the amazing map of Piri Reis that has mystified students of unexplained mysteries also involves Antarctica. The map shows mountain ranges in Antarctica, and lists the correct heights of various peaks. But because the land and its weather conditions are so harsh and severely cold, it was not until 1952 that scientists were able to penetrate the interior of Antarctica and study its mountain ranges at length. Their findings agreed with the Piri Reis map in every detail.

How could Piri Reis or anyone else alive in 1513 have possessed accurate information about mountain ranges and coastlines lying under ice in a land that no human had ever set eyes upon?

Several answers have been offered to explain the impossible accuracy of the Piri Reis map.

First, of course, the map could be a clever forgery. But it is not. Scientists have proven beyond any shadow of doubt that the map is genuine. Besides, some of the map's features were not proven to be correct until twenty years or more after the map was discovered.

Second, Piri Reis and his map-makers could have guessed at the locations and details of places they may have thought existed—or else they might have copied earlier maps which showed those sites. But in the former case their lucky "guesses" were so accurate, and so numerous, as to be literally impossible. And in the latter case, if they copied ancient maps, we are left with the even more difficult problem of how earlier map-makers could have known so much about unexplored coastlines and undiscovered lands.

Third, some people believe that thousands of years ago the earth was inhabited by a race of super-intelligent humans whose society was far superior to our own. According to this theory, these humans—who produced the Piri Reis map and other ancient maps (and could have been responsible for creating the Nazca Lines in Peru as well)—disappeared long ago without a trace. All that remains of their civilization is a handful of remarkably accurate maps, including the Piri Reis map.

A fourth theory holds that the map could have been prepared by aliens from outer space who were visiting Earth in the distant past. Before leaving, as a gesture of good will or friendship, they might have used their spacecraft and advanced technology to prepare highly accurate maps for use by the sea-going humans who remained behind when they left. The Piri Reis map could be one such map; as we have seen, it contains many details and features which were unknown in the 1500s when it was prepared. Another Turkish map, prepared in 1559, shows Antarctica and the western coast of the United States, but it also shows a land bridge between Russia and Alaska. This narrow strip of land connecting Russia to the U.S. does not exist now— the two countries are twenty miles apart, separated by the waters of the Bering Strait—but it did exist thirty thousand years ago, when our ancestors still lived in caves and hunted woolly mammoths!

Dead Ends · How high is up? How long is forever? What existed before time began? Is death an end or a beginning? Questions such as these have no answers that we know of. Try as we may, we cannot understand or explain everything in the universe. Some questions are nothing more than dead ends; that is, they simply have no answers.

And maybe some other questions were not meant to have answers that we can understand or explain.

If we walk by a full-length mirror, for example, we expect to see our reflection in the mirror. But what if, after passing the same mirror 62,563 times and seeing ourselves in its reflection every time, we pass by the mirror for the 62,564th time, in broad daylight and under normal conditions—only this time we aren't there in the mirror's reflection? How would we explain it?

Probably, we would sit down and try to develop a list of possible answers.

1. Our image was lost in the blank spot in our vision.

2. We weren't looking closely at the mirror at the time.

3. The room was dark.

4. The mirror has a flaw in it.

5. It must have been those diet pills we took.

But isn't that exactly the same thing we're doing in trying to understand and explain the amazing map of Piri Reis? We're trying to explain it in *our* terms, and as something natural, when in fact there is virtually nothing natural or normal about the map and the information it contains, except the men who drew it.

Maybe the Piri Reis map was meant to be *used*, not to be understood or explained. If so, we'll probably never know how it was created or why it is so accurate.

We'll still wonder about it, though. It is basic to human nature to question things, to search for answers and wonder about hows and whys, even when the questions lead us to dead ends.

THE SHROUD OF TURIN

THE SHROUD OF TURIN IS AN ANCIENT, YELLOWED LINEN CLOTH which measures fourteen feet long by three and a half feet wide. Many devout Christians believe that it is the burial cloth in which Jesus Christ was wrapped and laid in the tomb after His crucifixion by the Romans in 30 A.D. If so, it certainly is the most important single object in the Christian religion.

Other shrouds have been presented to the public as the authentic burial cloth of Jesus; what makes the Shroud of Turin unique—and mysterious—is that it bears the faint, but unmistakable, life-size image of a bearded white man with long hair. (In fact, it contains *two* images, head-to-head rather than side-by-side, indicating that the man was laid on his back on the shroud, which was then folded over to cover the front of his naked body.)

There's more, though. The ghostly, straw-colored images reveal that the man suffered savage wounds over much of his body before he died. These wounds correspond closely with Gospel accounts of the wounds inflicted on Jesus before and during His crucifixion.

Like the butcherous Nazis of Adolf Hitler's Germany in World War II, the ancient Romans were masters of cruelty and torture. Their beatings consisted of exactly forty lashes across the victim's body with a two-thonged whip, the ends of which were tipped with metal or bone to ensure maximum bleeding. Their favorite method of putting criminals to death was the slow agony of crucifixion: nailing the victim to a cross, and then waiting patiently for him to die.

According to New Testament accounts, Jesus suffered both of these tortures and more. To complete His humiliation, the Roman soldiers beat Him, placed a thorny crown upon His head, and then made Him carry a heavy wooden cross to the hill of Golgotha where He was to be crucified—a distance of more than half a mile.

The images on the Shroud of Turin show numerous bloody marks which appear to have been made by lashes. The wounds are concentrated most heavily around the man's chest, shoulders, back, and legs.

The images also show a series of blood-stained puncture wounds on the man's forehead and the back of his head—as if he had been forced to wear a crown of thorns. His ankles also show puncture wounds, as if they had been nailed to a cross.

A large, gaping wound in the man's left side is clearly visible in the image on the shroud. The wound, which is located between the man's fifth and sixth ribs, bears thick stains of blood and some unknown, colorless liquid. (This fact agrees with the text of *John* 16:34: "One of the soldiers with a spear pierced His side, and forthwith came there out blood and water.")

The man's right cheekbone is bruised and swollen, and his

right eyelid bears similar marks of injury, indicating that he had been beaten as well as scourged, or whipped. (Jesus was beaten twice: His beatings are described in *Matthew* 26:67 and 27:30.)

The man's shoulders, too, appear swollen and marked with cuts and bruises—as if, in the estimation of Dr. Robert Bucklin, the man had carried a rough object across his shoulders for a considerable length of time or distance in the hours just before his death. His knees have cuts and bruises which could have resulted from falling repeatedly, which suggests that the object he carried must have been extremely heavy.

Dr. Bucklin, who is a former assistant medical examiner for the county of Los Angeles, issued a report based on his study of photographs of the Shroud of Turin. He was particularly interested in a large, bloody puncture wound where the man's left hand and wrist joined. While Christians often speak of Jesus' "nail-scarred hands," the Roman method of crucifixion actually involved nailing the victim's wrists, not the palms of his hands, to the cross, since the fragile hands could not support the weight of a man's body on the cross. And because this fact was not common knowledge in the 1300s when the shroud first appeared publicly, Dr. Bucklin concluded that the wound was suffered by a man who had been crucified by the Romans. In Dr. Bucklin's professional estimation, the technical nature of the wounds shown on the Shroud of Turin "represents medical knowledge unknown 150 years ago." According to Dr. Bucklin, "The markings on this image are so clear and medically accurate that the [medical] facts they reflect are beyond dispute."

The front image shows the man's hands folded with his left hand on top of his right hand; thus, only the left hand shows the puncture wounds which would result from crucifixion. And to those who believe that the Shroud of Turin is a fake because the location of the puncture wound lies at the base of the hand rather than the palm, one can point out that the New Testament originally was written in Greek, and the ancient Greek word for "hand" —*cheir*—includes the wrist and forearm as well as the palm.

This is the outline of an interesting and perplexing puzzle: Is the Shroud of Turin the actual burial cloth in which Jesus was laid in the tomb belonging to Joseph of Arimathea, or is it a clever fake?

The last mention in the Gospels of the shroud occurs in *Luke* 24:12: "Then arose Peter [one of Jesus' disciples], and ran unto the sepulchre; and stooping down, he beheld the linen clothes laid by themselves, and departed."

After that, according to Christian tradition, the shroud was taken and hidden away by the early Christians for more than three hundred years. During that time the Romans fiercely persecuted and killed Christians as enemies of Rome and the emperor. The holy shroud ended up in the hands of the emperor in Constantinople; it remained there until Moslem invaders captured that city sometime around 1000 A.D.

Then, in 1204 A.D., the shroud was reclaimed by the Christian Crusaders from Europe when they recaptured Constantinople from the Moslems. The Crusaders carried the shroud home with them to Europe where, in 1353, it entered the possession of a Frenchman, Geoffrey de Charney. He displayed the shroud to worshippers as "the true Shroud of our Lord."

Many years later, de Charney's daughter presented the shroud as a gift to an Italian nobleman—Louis, Duke of Savoy. It remained in the duke's palace until, in 1532, it was damaged in a fire that destroyed the chapel in which it was kept. Servants managed to save the shroud, but it was burned slightly around the edges. (These burned areas have since been patched.) Water that was poured on the shroud to put out the fire left a series of large, permanent water stains on the cloth.

After the fire, the shroud was moved to the Cathedral of St.

John the Baptist in Turin, Italy. It has been there ever since, except for a brief period during World War II when it was moved to another part of Italy in order to protect it from bombing raids.

The shroud is kept under close guard and strict security in a silver chest within the cathedral. It is presently owned by the Vatican, which is the ruling body of the Catholic Church. The shroud is shown publicly only about four times each century. Whenever it is displayed, it draws thousands of Christian pilgrims from all over the world. They believe that in its images they are seeing the Man whose simple teachings changed the world: Jesus of Nazareth, the Son of God.

Is the Shroud a Forgery? · Ever since the shroud was first publicly displayed in the fourteenth century in France as "the true Shroud of our Lord," people have wondered if it is the actual burial cloth in which Jesus' body was wrapped. Arguments for and against its authenticity have raged back and forth for six hundred years.

These arguments center around a single question: How did the image get on the shroud in the first place?

Those people who contend that the Shroud of Turin is a cleverly contrived fake say that the image was painted on— probably by a clever and talented artist during the Middle Ages—or else it was scorched on by draping the cloth over a statue which was heated sufficiently to burn an image onto its surface.

Those who insist that the shroud is real accept the Gospel account of Jesus' burial following Jewish customs of the times: "And there came also Nicodemus . . . and brought a mixture of myrrh and aloes, about an hundred pound weight. Then they took the body of Jesus, and wound it in linen clothes with the spices, as the manner of the Jews is to bury" (*John* 19:39–40). Thus, believers contend that the image on the shroud resulted from contact with perspiration on Jesus' body mixed with the oils and spices in which His body was wrapped.

Of course, the best way to prove or disprove these theories is to test them scientifically. Such tests were in fact conducted in 1959, 1970, 1973, and 1978, using millions of dollars' worth of the latest and most advanced scientific equipment.

The results of these tests, which were conducted by teams of specialists including art historians, Bible scholars, photographic specialists, textile experts, chemists, physicists, and many other scientific experts, are startling almost beyond belief.

These experts discovered that *all three of the previous theories are wrong*. None of these things—not paint nor fire nor burial oils—could have produced the man's image that appears on the Shroud of Turin.

The broadest study ever undertaken of the shroud was done in 1978 by a team of fifty U.S. scientists and experts. They traveled to Turin, Italy, and studied the shroud thoroughly for five days, using more than six tons of scientific equipment. After that, they and three hundred fifty other scientists spent more than two years analyzing the data they had collected. Their statements and findings included the following:

• The image on the shroud is a negative image, like the negatives you get with photographs when you have a roll of film developed. But the cloth itself is known to be at least five hundred years older than photography. Could an artist from the Middle Ages have produced a painting in negative form when there was no such thing at the time?

• The cloth is old-ivory linen, well preserved although yellowed with age. It has permanent, deep crease marks from being kept folded in the past. The linen contains traces of a kind of cotton that is found in the Middle East. Its threads were spun by hand and bleached before weaving, as was the Hebrew custom of the times. No one knows for sure if the cloth is two thousand years old, since the Archbishop of Turin will not permit the kind of testing (known as carbon-dating) that could reveal the shroud's actual age.

However, the 1973 tests showed that the cloth was woven in a herringbone pattern that was sometimes used in ancient Palestine. The scientists also found, in studying the shroud under a microscope, that it contained tiny spores of a type of pollen that was (and is) found in Palestine where Jesus lived.

• The image was *not* painted on. No trace of any sort of paint or dye was found on the cloth, even when viewed under a high-powered microscope. Besides, if the image had been painted on, the paint or dye would have run when the shroud was soaked with water in the fire of 1532.

Dr. John Jackson, a physicist at the U.S. Air Force Academy who was one of the fifty scientists who traveled to Italy in 1978 to study the shroud, said, "As scientists, we believe it would be impossible for a forger, much less [one who lived in the Middle Ages], to have produced an image like this."

• The image was *not* scorched on—at least, not in the way we expect scorching to occur. When viewed under a microscope, the image seems to lie on top of the fiber tips, whereas either painting or scorching would have penetrated the fibers. And if the cloth had been draped over a hot statue to produce scorch marks, high spots (like the nose) where the cloth touched the statue would be darker than other areas where the shroud did not come into direct contact with the statue. Yet the darkness of the two images is constant. It does not vary anywhere on the shroud.

• The same factor applies to the possible mixture of body oils, spices, and perspiration to account for the images. Traces of one such chemical—aloe—were found on the shroud; still, that could not account for places where the body did not touch the

cloth. This is particularly true of the face and neck, where the shroud image shows fine details which should not have appeared on the cloth. (If this is unclear, try lying under a sheet in your bed tonight, playing dead. If you do this, you'll find that the sheet does not touch certain parts of your face such as your eyes, or other areas of your body such as your neck and the small of your back.)

• The bloodstains found on the shroud are real. They are composed of hemoglobin, which is the agent in blood that gives it its red color. The blood is human blood.

• The shroud shows no signs of mold or mildew, despite its being stored in many damp or musty places over the years. Scientists believe that the lack of mold or mildew may be due to certain ancient Hebrew cloth-making techniques.

• According to the best scientific estimation, the image on the Shroud of Turin occurred, not as the result of direct contact, but rather by some unknown kind of energy projection which could have acted at a distance. What form this energy projection might be, scientists cannot even guess.

• According to a prepared statement issued by members of the Shroud of Turin Research Project, which conducted the 1978 study, "We can conclude that the Shroud image is that of a real, human form, of a scourged, crucified man. It is not the product of an artist."

One researcher, Dr. John Lynn of the NASA Jet Propulsion Laboratory, declared that "It would be miraculous if it were a forgery."

Believers in the shroud as the burial cloth of Jesus Christ have their own answer to the question, *What caused the image?* They believe the force that projected the image onto the Shroud of Turin is the same force that raised Him from the dead: the power of God.

But is the image on the shroud that of Jesus Christ? Science cannot help us here. As one Research Project member put it, "We do not have a [scientific] test for Jesus Christ."

Still, experts have estimated that the odds *against* another man's receiving wounds identical to those suffered by Jesus, as described in the four Gospels of the New Testament and shown on the Shroud of Turin, are something like 250 billion to 1. (To get an idea of what this figure means, consider that, in all of human history, only sixty-five billion people have ever lived; and less than sixty-two billion seconds have ticked on the clock since Jesus' death.)

What all this means is that, if the Shroud of Turin is genuine, then its image almost certainly *is* that of Jesus Christ. And if it's *not* genuine—it's a forgery that has completely fooled many of the greatest scientific minds and the most sophisticated scientific equipment that exist on earth today.